D1259838

BOOKS & BATTLES

AMERICAN LITERATURE: 1920–1930

AN EDITOR UNDER ARREST

H. L. Mencken (*left*) beams upon Police Lieutenant Dan Hines after
being arrested for selling *The American Mercury* in Boston

BOOKS & BATTLES

BATTLES

AMERICAN LITERATURE, 1920—1930

IRENE AND ALLEN CLEATON

COOPER SQUARE PUBLISHERS, INC.
NEW YORK
1970

For

EMMA WHITTON CLEATON
SUNSET BREUCHAUD HASBROOK
CHARLES PHILLIPS HASBROOK

CONTENTS

ILLUSTRATIONS

BRIEFLY INTRODUCTORY

IT IS one of the sadnesses of life that literary histories if they are comprehensive are also as dull as year before last's baseball scores. The typical account of the literature of a period is principally a catalogue of names, titles, and dates. So-and-so wrote this-and-that in such-and-such a year. It was Tragedy, or Comedy, or Satire. Or maybe the chronicler undertakes impressive classifications, like Romance and Realism, and gets lost climbing the curves and spirals of trends. In either case his book is likely to be the kind considered suitable for college students, and read by nobody else. Too much of the blame for the average American's shrinking from the 'classics' is put upon the sixth-grade teacher who tells her pupils Longfellow was a great poet and upon the junior high pedagogue who, trying to beguile adolescents into reading *The Mill on the Floss*, maintains that it is a great novel. The professors deserve their share of censure, too, for presenting literature's 'background' of facts to college boys and girls in textbooks that have all the spontaneity, gaiety, and insight of a grocery boy's order book.

This is not to suggest that the authors of this history of American literature from 1920 to 1930 lay any claim to spontaneity, gaiety, and insight. Still less is it to hint that the book should be adopted as a textbook. It is too informal, too anecdotal, in general too journalistic, for that.

Moreover, the book undertakes to report on the new treatment of sex and the tendency toward bawdiness and profanity which were characteristic of the period. And the colleges have not yet carried into the lecture hall the frankness of the laboratory in biology.

What we do want to emphasize is that this book is not a 'complete' literary history of the 'twenties. It omits mention of many writers who possessed some measure of worth. There is no attempt to give a full list of the books of any single author. The reviewer may base an indignant column on the fact that this book or that writer is not included. To have precluded such criticism it would have been necessary only to rewrite *Who's Who in America*, with some assistance from the publicity departments of the publishers.

This did not seem worth while; on the contrary, it seemed distinctly inadvisable. For our purpose was to present the significant facts in as lively a manner as our talents permitted. We have tried to strike a mean between the entertaining and the important, with, of course, the hope of being as accurate as any professor: Mussey is not our model, but neither is Herodotus. We are interested, and it is our hope that our readers will be interested, less in the date of a writer's birth than in the manner in which he lived after that date. We are interested not only in the books that were sold in Boston, but in those that were suppressed there — and in the whole story of the fight on censorship, which was won during the decade and which appeared to be worth a chapter in itself. It seems to us that the list of the best-sellers of the decade is less revealing than a discussion of why certain ones were best-sellers.

We have made no effort to explore the vast fields of poetry and the drama, confining ourselves to what literary editors label 'fiction' and 'non-fiction,' but we have discussed rather fully the Little Magazines, the expatriate movement, the limited edition fad, and a score of other subjects that appeared to be diverting and, for divers reasons, significant. If this eclecticism seems to the reader undesirable, he is hereby formally warned.

A NOTE IN CONTRAST

THE nineteen-twenties were the most exciting decade in American literature. About us crackled the lightning of Dadaism, the Young Intellectuals, the New Humanism, the Negro artists, the Lively Arts. Writing men and women were in a fever of revolt against tradition and the limitations under which they lived and worked. The writer stepped from the seclusion of his library into the turmoil of social, economic, and political movements, risking jail by thumbing his nose at the censors and sometimes actually going there for taking part in 'demonstrations' against authority. In the limelight were men of heady ideas like F. Scott Fitzgerald, Waldo Frank, Ernest Boyd, Sinclair Lewis, Joseph Wood Krutch, Ernest Hemingway, Edmund Wilson, Lewis Mumford, Gilbert Seldes, and James Branch Cabell. They wrote not of the triumph of nobility and virtue, as their American predecessors had done, but of sex, disillusionment, escape, the younger generation, the horror of life in small towns, the hypocrisy of American business and government, Victorianism, Puritanism, the stupidity of the habits and notions of the middle-aged and the elderly....

But first it may be amusing and worth while to glance at what went before. In the light of the turbulent decade which followed, one looks back upon the 1919 literary scene with something akin to the vague incredulity with which we now regard the far-off days of prohibition. In that year Robert W. Chambers, then one of the most highly paid concocters of literary narcotics for the multitude, was interviewed on the state of American literature. In those days people talked of the forthcoming Great American Novel as ministers spoke of the Second Coming. For a reporter interviewing a novelist not to have asked him about the Great American Novel would have been as unorthodox as, a few years later, it would have been not to get a visiting European's opinion of bobbed hair. The reporter varied the formula by asking Chambers whether he thought the West was more likely than the East to produce the Great American Novel. Chambers replied:

> I think not. We in the East have lost a little of our raw self-consciousness. The West seems to have lost none, so far. Many of us have forgotten that we happen to live east of the Mississippi. But the West has, so far, forgotten nothing. 'East is East and West is West,' and there's no earthly reason why the twain shouldn't meet, mingle, and merge, and take it for granted that it's all the same bunch and that 'the gang's all here.' But the West is always busy marking out the boundary which we never notice until our attention is called to it. And it rather bores us.

If this interview had appeared in a small-town newspaper, it would not, at this date, be worth recalling. It is conceivable that a city editor somewhere might have considered Chambers of sufficient weight as a writer to be interviewed on American literature, and that his smug, superficial judgments, his barbarous handling of the language, might have been printed.

But this interview was published in the leading literary organ of the country, *The Bookman*. Its appearance offers a hint of the state of the art in 1919 — on the supine editorial worship of popular success that then prevailed, on the listless tempo of the march of ideas, on the absence of excitement in the world of books, on the poverty of critical ideas.

They were dull days. A survey which showed that the most popular authors among the inmates of insane asylums were George Barr McCutcheon, Harold Bell Wright, Chambers, and Harold MacGrath might well have been a survey of the reading habits of the sane as well. The most talked-of book of the year, and the best-seller by all odds, was Wright's *The Re-creation of Brian Kent*, a bloodless tale with many morals. The most interesting gossip concerned the question whether Miss Daisy Ashford had really written *The Young Visiters* when she was nine years old, or whether Sir James Barrie had written it when he was fifty-nine. The big literary news was the sale of the motion-picture rights of *Pollyanna* for a production by Mary Pickford, the payment of sixty-five thousand dollars for the memoirs of General von Ludendorff, who was to be advertised as 'the worst man in the world,' and the appearance in an article by Richard

Wright of the don't-give-him-a-book-he's-got-a-book gag.

Joseph Hergesheimer, now a successful writer who had broken into print with a recipe for stuffed cabbage which he sold to *Good Housekeeping* under the name of his wife, complained in a magazine article against the assumption, 'typical of our high-minded fiction, that virtue and poverty are one,' and correctly summarized the case when he stated that 'our most widely circulated fiction very accurately carries our peculiar national defects — an easy sentimentality, pretentiousness, an avoidance of meeting truth squarely, and an almost complete confusion of prudery and purity.'

Henry Litchfield West, then a popular writer on literature, told us that 'children need books to supply the foundation of intelligent patriotism.' One of the most highly regarded books of 1919 was Doctor Henry van Dyke's *The Valley of Vision*, the most startling idea of which was that 'the Mountain-Top is the place of outlook over the earth and the sea. But it is in the valley of suffering, endurance, and self-sacrifice that the deeper visions of the meaning of life come to us.' A characteristic performance was the production of a book of stories by various writers who set out to catch 'the wit and interest of Boccaccio without his naughtiness.' Among the best-selling American books of the year were Gouverneur Morris's *The Wild Goose*, Frances Hodgson Burnett's *The Good Wolf*, and Gene Stratton-Porter's *Homing with the Birds*.

The critics, for the most part, had little to say that was arresting, save for a few who had not yet found either themselves or the necessary audience. H. L. Mencken was an exception. His witty lashings of the academicians were gradually winning readers. But Heywood Broun was just beginning to make the literary section of the New York *Tribune* interesting. Burton Rascoe and Harry Hansen were comparatively unknown outside a small group in Chicago. John Farrar had not become editor of *The Bookman.* Ernest Boyd was a British vice-consul in Baltimore. Floyd Dell had published only *Women as World-Builders* and *Were You Ever a Child?* Gilbert Seldes was an associate editor of *Collier's.*

A fairly typical criticism was that of Constance Murray Greene, who reviewed a book called *The Man Who Discovered Himself,* by Willis George Emerson. Emerson's tale was of a man who works to support an extravagant wife and daughter until his health is ruined, gets a job as a cobbler, saves a little money, goes West, becomes wealthy, and returns home to hear his unrecognizing wife denounce him as a 'terrible man.' Passing judgment on this sentimental, flabby, obvious story, Miss Greene rejoiced that the wife failed to recognize her husband when he returned, for 'it saved him from her toils, and he is the one nearest our hearts.'

RUMBLINGS AND A PROPHECY

THERE were, of course, faint rumblings of what was to come when the boys home from the war and the army camps emerged with the books which they were at the moment writing. Clarence Budington Kelland, before lapsing into respectability as a contributor to the successful 'success' magazine, *The American*, wrote a story called *The Little Moment of Happiness* in which American girls approved of their soldier friends having affairs with French *midinettes*. Sherwood Anderson produced his groping, poetic *Winesburg, Ohio*. Grant Overton, the Barnum of American literature, computed there was an audience of at least fifteen thousand for 'novels in which the esthetic or artistic quality is predominant,' and that this audience might reach one hundred and fifty thousand if a book 'possesses something beyond merely beautiful art.' And an anonymous and extraordinarily sensitive critic detected in the literary tempo 'a nervousness that is unrestful, a state of perpetual motion and emotion, a Saint Vitus dance movement.'

But only Joseph Hergesheimer foresaw with clarity and completeness what demobilization was to mean in the world of literature. In the summer of 1919 he looked into the crystal and wrote:

> Here was a most extraordinary and new audience, a public clear-eyed and critical, supremely invigorating.... A great many trivialities had been blotted from their interests and needs... they were forever lost to the purely superficial.... I saw them [the writers] penetrating the entire fabric of American life and exposing, with the acid of their supreme experience, countless rotten threads and false designs.

Here, in brief, was a new generation.

I. SUNRISE GUN

I. SUNRISE GUN

Here was a new generation, shouting the old cries, learning the old creeds, through a revery of long days and nights; destined finally to go out into that dirty gray turmoil to follow love and pride; a new generation dedicated more than the last to the fear of poverty and the worship of success; grown up to find all Gods dead, all wars fought, all faiths in man shaken...

F. Scott Fitzgerald: *This Side of Paradise*

IF THE literature of the 'twenties can be described in a phrase, that phrase is revolt against Puritanism and Victorianism.

Fortunately it was a great deal more. We have it on the word of Ernest Boyd that in the decade American literature 'grew up.' And there is (or was) the quite tangible $46,350 which Sinclair Lewis received as the Nobel Prize to prove American literature had become a World Force. In detail, there were a number of thrillingly fine literary performances which were worthy of at least a part of the acclaim they got from a not very critical generation, without reference to any quality of revolt inherent in them.

But the authors who did the most striking work in the decade were busily and rather stridently in revolt against some facet or other of those dread philosophies which were loosely described as Victorianism and Puritanism — against the taboo of mentioning sexual intercourse, against the reactionarism of parents who objected to seventeen-

year-old girls drinking bad liquor all night at speakeasies and coming home the next morning in evening
dresses, against the naïve idea of the middle-aged and
the elderly that there might be a place for them in the
world.

Early in the decade Puritanism lost the old definition
inherent in the cartoon of a gaunt preacher in a long black
coat and a stovepipe hat with a Bible under one arm and
an umbrella under the other. It ceased to be merely the
enemy of the pleasures against which primitive, evangelical Christianity had always crusaded — dancing, card-
playing, drinking, profanity, and blasphemy. It objected, or was assumed to object, to the license of life and
literature that was peculiar to the period — 'necking,'
young women in short skirts sliding down banisters, the
use of the phrase 'son-of-a-bitch' in books, the new
freedom under which parties to a marriage 'lived their
own lives' (definition: being unfaithful), and such printed
observations as James Branch Cabell's that 'breakage' is
connected with the loss of a woman's virginity, but not a
man's. And so Puritanism came to be something to put
down violently, forever, and by any means that might be
effective.

> 'If Plymouth Rock had landed on the Pilgrims,
> Instead of the Pilgrims landing on the rock,'

sang Raymond Hitchcock to the satisfied laughter of
audiences at the 1921 Ziegfeld Follies, and F. Scott Fitzgerald wrote:

> 'Victorians, Victorians, who never learned to weep,
> Who sowed the bitter harvest that your children go to reap.'

They were twin enemies. Victorianism represented calmness, poise, the use of 'limbs' instead of 'legs' or 'stems,' avoidance of sex as a topic in literature or conversation, ignorance of Freud, patriotism. It had, so far as its contemners revealed, no precise definition. Whatever exponents of literary freedom and looseness in manners hated was dismissed as a relic of Victorianism, if it had not already been classified as Puritanism. But if the word was not defined, there was concerning it one absolute certainty: in the 'twenties it was always uttered in a tone of contempt. The objection to the Victorians went to such lengths that Fitzgerald complained bitterly that they 'took fifty years of Europe,' in spite of the historical fact that they drove out no lovelier settlers in order to live there. When Richard Le Gallienne remarked that after all Wordsworth, Morris, Rossetti, Swinburne, Darwin, Huxley, Tyndall, Newman, and Shaw were Victorians, no one paid any attention. Le Gallienne retorted that the writings of the 'supercilious and modish' detractors of Victorianism reminded him of puppies misbehaving against the pyramids, and subsided into a silence which the new generation was forcing upon all its elders in the literary world.

For the new generation ruled the roost. The shoutings of H. L. Mencken, learned and violent, became the critical voice of America. The younger newspaper critics, equipped with a knowledge of all the superlatives in the language and little else, echoed in a hundred places the points of view which he frankly called prejudices. Mencken was against authority, and authority was represented by the professors. Whatever the professors said was cried

down — and most of the professors were handicapped by
the fact that they neither wrote as well nor knew as much
as the Baltimore Anti-Christ. In the editorial chairs as
well as in the newspaper critical berths, young men pre-
dominated. Even in business the hard-pressed middle-
aged began to grant that some mystic competence resided
in youth. Young men were constantly remarking that it
was the older people who had got us into the horrible
stupidity of the World War, and the accusation was as
hard to answer as their frequent observation that, after
all, they had not asked to be born.

BLASTS AGAINST THE ELDERS

THE sunrise gun of the nineteen-twenties was a three-
barreled volley. The men behind it were Cabell, Fitzgerald, and Sinclair Lewis. *Main Street* and *This Side of
Paradise* came out in 1920, and *Jurgen*, though it left the
presses in the latter part of 1919, got little attention from
anybody but Mencken and Burton Rascoe, to whom it
was dedicated, until the first year of the decade. Lewis,
who had been potboiling for the *Saturday Evening Post* for
some time, was no youngster home from the wars, nor was
Cabell, who in his rural retreat near what he prefers to call
Richmond-in-Virginia had been writing charming medieval romances for years. But their books were as surely
aimed against what the Elders stood for, as clearly in-

tended for consumption by the younger generation who were being nonconformists by conforming to a hatred of Victorianism and Puritanism, as that of Fitzgerald, who was in his early twenties.

The three books were the most revolutionary American literature had produced. They warred on the sacred Americanisms that sex was to be discussed in writing only in small boys' scribblings on pavements, that residents in small towns were more admirable than those in wicked metropolitan centers, and that the political, economic, and social notions that had prevailed before the war were impregnable to successful attack. Their appearance cut a sharp dichotomy in American literature. It recognized the existence of a new and very different reading public. It offered the younger rebels flags and drums and bugles which sounded a call to arms against everything that in their restlessness and pugnacity they had grown to despise.

All these books sold widely and to an extravagantly admiring public, but they did not drive the more conventional, the less iconoclastic productions from the stalls. Save for their emergence, and that of a few faintly comparable works, the literary scene of 1920 bore a familiar appearance. The best-seller list included the memoirs of Princess Eugénie, whose name was later to be connected with a plumed, tri-cornered hat. The most popular books of the year were Peter B. Kyne's *Kindred of the Dust*, Kathleen Norris's *Harriet and the Piper*, Ethel M. Dell's *The Top of the World*, James Oliver Curwood's *The Valley of Silent Men*, Zane Grey's *The Man of the Forest*, and Harold Bell Wright's *The Re-creation of Brian Kent*,

all of them without literary distinction and none even re-
motely concerned with revolt. Jewel-studded Vincente
Blasco Ibañez, whose *The Four Horsemen of the Apocalypse*
had brought him money, and Rudolph Valentino money
and fame also, came over to lecture as the publishers
brought out his *Enemies of Women*. Sir Arthur Whitten
Brown produced the first of the popular books on aviation
with *Flying the Atlantic in Sixteen Hours*. A pious book
called *The Art of Pleasing Men* appeared, to the acclaim of
the cloth. And Octavus Roy Cohen continued to bank
huge sums made on stories about Negroes which showed
no understanding of Negroes at all.

Between the extremes of run-of-the-mine writing and
intelligent iconoclasm were a few books done well and in
a sound and academically acceptable tradition. Willa
Cather, an excellent craftsman with a disciplined imagination, reprinted a volume of short stories called *Youth and
the Bright Medusa* which proved her to be a better artist
than Frances Newman, who jeered at her for tatting of an
evening at the MacDowell Art Colony, said a person with
such prosaic ideas of entertainment could possibly be.
Joseph Hergesheimer, with some years to go before he
would write a sexy story of the country club set called
Cytherea, turned out a lovely story of a beautiful and
defeated woman named, as was her biography, *Linda Condon*. Linda, who cherished her beauty as a pianist would
the suppleness of his wrists, was a cold and virginal
woman, and although the tale which presented her to the
American public was the best of Hergesheimer's books,
there was not enough sex for any great hand-clapping on
the part of the public. A few critics cheered, and Cabell

wrote a beautiful and adulatory review, but when the book reached the best-seller list in Illinois, North Dakota, and Wisconsin, one felt that it had gone quite as far toward popularity as could have been expected.

FIRECRACKERS IN PARADISE

ACROSS a horizon only beginning to be brightened as news of Cabell's *Jurgen* got about, and kept visible by the glow from Hergesheimer's *Linda Condon*, flashed, in April of 1920, the hot, bright comet which Fitzgerald called *This Side of Paradise.*

It is rather difficult to imagine any book today creating the furor which *This Side of Paradise* did. It was certainly not, on the whole, well written. There were passages that had the poetical quality of Swinburne and stretches of dialogue that were smoothly 'natural.' But there were also long sections that were pedestrian, uninspired, downright dull. The book was jerky, disjointed, episodic, marred by misused words, bad spelling, and mystifying grammar. In spite of all that, it was instantly acclaimed by the only critics worthy of the name in America, and admired in the upper brackets of the reading public. It had a quality that was quite fresh and original, and one cannot read it even today, when its sense of timeliness has faded, without feeling it is a truly extraordinary book.

Fitzgerald, a wealthy, good-looking Middle-Westerner,

began the book after leaving Princeton for an officers' training camp. Under the light of army lanterns, seated on cracker boxes in tents, he worked on it when the day's drilling was done. The Armistice came before *The Romantic Egoist*, as the book then was to be called, was finished. The war, which drove John Dos Passos to write his bitter *Three Soldiers* and the crippled Laurence Stallings to the evangelical disillusionment of *Plumes* and the play *What Price Glory?* was to Fitzgerald only a romantic interlude. He returned to civilian clothes and rewrote the book just as it would have been written if what he called the 'delayed Teutonic migration' had not been begun.

Briefly, it is the story of a poetic, intellectual, 'smooth' young man named Amory Blaine, who goes to a good prep school, misses distinction at Princeton, writes a few poems about the war, falls in love, is jilted, and in the end of the book, broke and baffled and rootless, is flirting with the idea of embracing Socialism, the political faith of Fitzgerald. An obvious enough theme, not particularly distinguished by good writing or craftsmanship.

What gave it its breathless quality, what made it the testament of American youth, what made its author the idol of all the flappers of the day? The answer is very simple: *This Side of Paradise* was a cry of revolt. It championed youth as against the old, the rebels against the conformists. It presented the arguments of the young plausibly and ingratiatingly. It endowed them with an intelligence and with learning which, in the nature of things, most of them did not possess. It dignified their philosophy. It encouraged them in defying their elders and following their freest desires. It cast over their doings and dreams a wistful, poetic, and nostalgic haze.

H. G. Wells once said a novel had to introduce a female character within the first ten pages to be successful. In the 'twenties the novelist had to be mathematically certain of another recommendation — he had to mention Freud. An essayist of the period said one discovered Freud in the 'twenties as once one had discovered God. Readers of *This Side of Paradise* discovered Freud on page six, and the book was as up-to-date in every other respect. Beatrice, Amory's mother, was a sot, but she was made out to be infinitely glamorous.

There was a strong contempt for the Victorians and, because Mencken had finally succeeded in getting an American audience for him, a flavor of Nietzsche. Amory was contemptuous of the bourgeoisie, democracy, and American life, which was 'so damned dumb and stupid and healthy.' He talked about petting and used the word '*simpatico*' and confused his elders with his brilliant conversation. He was properly shocking by showing an amused tolerance at his father's funeral.

And, as Dwight Fiske would say, they *loved* it! By the end of the year *This Side of Paradise* topped every best-seller list in the country. The book had been rejected by five publishers before Maxwell Perkins of Scribner's accepted it by special delivery, but now Fitzgerald found himself deluged by requests for magazine stories. He wrote several, including the strange 'Diamond as Big as the Ritz' for *Smart Set*, being edited by Mencken and George Jean Nathan, and achieved the goal of all short story writers who are not well heeled: he became a regular contributor to the *Saturday Evening Post*. The critics, led by Mencken, joined the chorus that arose from the campuses.

> His books [wrote Sidney Howard in 1921] were a nine days' wonder with the critics. To us the novel seems the clearest treatment of American youth in any fiction of recent years. We like the flagrant disregard of formula which throws the book from conventional narrative to short story, drama in dialogue, and even to extremely interesting passages in verse.... He is possessed of a fine sense of the significant beauty of things.... His novel would have been better had he written it later in his life, but it would have been less true.

Fitzgerald's book deserves this praise, but that its popularity was not due entirely to the qualities noted by Howard seems proved by the fact that his contemporaries, who lacked his high literary talent but shared his philosophy of youth and knew how to be shocking, were almost as widely read. An example was Dorothy Speare, an ambitious singer turned writer, who, to her annoyance, was called the 'F. Scott Fitzgeraldine of American literature.' In *The Gay Year* (1923) Miss Speare shows us the country club set, with the youngsters behaving so wildly the older members start a separate club. She tells us of the invasion of a private club by non-members who 'borrow' bathing-suits and use the private beach for a party, of a club dance with the 'neckers' downstairs, of women becoming addicts of craps-shooting, of a girl standing on a table to sing 'The Face on the Barroom Floor,' of young people carrying a real estate sign to a cemetery and drinking among the tombstones. Typical Speare conversation: 'You don't see much of this love-in-a-cottage stuff any more, or starting-out-on-what-he-first-earns. Their ideas have grown expensive and large, and have elbowed love aside.' . . . 'You spit a bibful,' said a well-born Boston debutante. . . . 'Life was as flat as stale coffee grounds.'

Fitzgerald wrote some stories which offered little besides sensationalism. As in his first novel, he catered to the poses of the very young and badly behaved, but he did it with little of the literary graces that distinguished the biography of Amory Blaine. In 'Bernice Bobs Her Hair' he tells us that Marjorie Harvey was 'justly celebrated for having turned five cart-wheels in succession during the last pump-and-slipper dance at New Haven,' that 'the idea of fox-trotting more than one full fox-trot with the same girl is distasteful, not to say odious,' and that 'these days it's every girl for herself.'

But Fitzgerald did not succumb completely to the easy money of the slick-paper magazines and the tinsel magnificence of Hollywood. With a new fortune at his feet, he sailed for France, and, with interludes of fiction of varying quality for the *Saturday Evening Post*, began working on a novel which was to go far beyond the sparkling improvisation of *This Side of Paradise* and *The Beautiful and the Damned*, which had followed. After years of work, dark uncertainty, and manuscripts that were begun only to be destroyed, he was to produce in *The Great Gatsby* one of the brightest literary ornaments of the latter part of the decade.

A REFORMER FROM MAIN STREET

IF FITZGERALD was satisfied to talk ironically of the American scene and then to flee to the warm, tender nights of the Rue Pigalle, Sinclair Lewis was belligerent enough about the American scene to be determined to do something about it. By the time 'Doodles' Lewis, a Middle-Western child of a family of physicians, had become 'Red' Lewis and a Yale man, he was already something of a reformer. He could become eloquent in criticism of the capitalistic system, though less amusing and devastating than he was when he mimicked the political and ecclesiastical pundits of the day, and he admired the new Utopias of economists and politicians. He might have become a preacher, a politician, a single taxer, a Social Credit Man, the organizer of the Doctor Townsend Club of Sauk Center, Minnesota. He became a novelist.

As a reporter in New Haven and San Francisco and the editor of the red-blooded *Adventure Magazine*, he had little opportunity to reform institutions or people. His first book, *Our Mr. Wrenn*, published the year Americans learned of the existence of Sarajevo, was conventional enough. *The Trail of the Hawk*, *The Job*, and *Free Air*, brought out between 1914 and 1920, added little to his literary fame, but increased his bank balance to the two thousand dollars which he had decided he needed to take a year off from potboiling to write a 'serious novel.' The idea for this novel, to be called *The Village Virus* and

to show how the stultifying and insidious influence of a
small town kept a potentially great lawyer from winning
to the fame and fortune that should have been his, had
been fermenting in his restless mind for fifteen years.
Taking the two thousand dollars, a part of *The Village
Virus*, and enough of his conception of the lawyer character to create Guy Pollack, Lewis went to Washington,
D.C., and wrote *Main Street*.

It is estimated that three million persons have read
Main Street. Within a few months after its publication,
it headed the best-seller list, and it remained there, unchallenged, for nearly a year. It was debated, denounced,
praised almost with reverence, translated, and imitated.
It introduced a new phrase into our language. It made
the entire nation aware of its shortcomings and irksomely
self-conscious. It gave Europeans, suffering from the
hangover of wartime adulation of America, a tonic dose
of tomato juice.

Main Street is the story of the revolt of Carol Milford,
an idealistic and somewhat arty young reformer just out
of college, against the Gopher Prairie of Doctor Will
Kennicott, whom she married partly because she was in
love, partly because she was tired of working, and partly
because she thought of Gopher Prairie as an inanimate
guinea pig of convenient size for her laboratory experiments in city planning, child welfare, and General Culture.
The book, which runs to 451 pages of small type, is the
story of the slow collapse of her idealism, the defeat of her
unselfishness by the pettiness, the meanness, and the
provinciality of a typical small town.

Carol was constantly in revolt, and because her revolt

was not merely against the standards of the small Middle-Western town, but against the standards which Americans — North, East, South, and West — could recognize as American, the book was pressed close to the bosom of the public.

Lewis, whose novel was refreshingly written and full of immensely capable reporting, had achieved the dual aims of nourishing and encouraging the *révoltés*, thus catering to his stomach, and gratifying his desire to reform, thus catering to his soul. His bold and accurate analysis of the village virus caused a self-examination, a soul-searching throughout the land that unquestionably made life pleasanter for the Carol Kennicotts, the Vida Sherwins, the Fern Mullinses, and the Raymie Wutherspoons who are condemned to live far from picture galleries, theaters, and decent libraries, among people whose conversation never rises above talk of babies, inner tubes, and the Biblical lore of the new pastor. Lewis's major *tour de force* in reform, *Babbitt*, was not to come until after his trip to Europe, but when he went to England and met George Moore, his literary hero, he could boast to the author who kissed and told that his college dreams had not been completely unfulfilled. He had made the world a little better.

UNMORAL MAGICKING IS CENSORED

THE zeal for reform which animated Lewis was totally absent from the makeup of James Branch Cabell, whose sole desire, as he frequently told the world, was to 'write perfectly of beautiful happenings.' Cabell, of whom the tabloid newspaper phrase 'member of an aristocratic Virginia family' is really true, has attempted to do little else during his life. As a boy in his Richmond-in-Virginia he devoured books and experimented in prose while the other boys were playing leap-frog and mumblety-peg, and by the time he was seventeen his prose style was so formed that it is almost indistinguishable from his style at the peak of his career. At the College of William and Mary in Williamsburg, called Fairhaven in his books, the young Cabell and a friend learned to drink alcohol straight, and wrote almost the entire students' literary magazine — poems, fiction, essays, and book reviews. Cabell signed his name only to news reports of the activities of his fraternity, Kappa Alpha, but under obvious pseudonyms were to be found poems that he later reprinted in *From the Hidden Way* and whole chapters, with hardly a word changed, that were to appear in *Beyond Life* when he was forty.

Cabell put in a few years on newspapers, leaving his initials carved on the reporters' desk in police court in Richmond for the inspiration of coming generations of ambitious young cubs, and produced a few works of genealogy, but he did not work for a living very long. He settled down to write perfectly of beautiful happenings, free of the necessity of catering to the tastes of either editors or the public. The public ignored him, and the editors interfered only to the extent of asking him to change the word 'belly' in a short story to 'stomach.' He seemed destined to be a writer of whom only a few thousand readers would ever hear.

Then came *Jurgen*. Denied the sales of *Main Street* and *This Side of Paradise*, for the reason that it was put into coventry by the New York Society for the Suppression of Vice and read by thousands in borrowed copies, this 'Comedy of Justice,' as it was subtitled, ranked with them in influence. Where Fitzgerald had mocked at an older, muddled generation and Lewis had scorned American folkways, Cabell went the whole hog and ridiculed notions and prejudices that were universal. His Jurgen, riding on a centaur and clad in a magic shirt, visited heaven, hell, and the bed-chambers of more lovely ladies than one ordinarily meets in a lifetime. He discussed our notions of domestic felicity, our standards of morals, and our political conceptions with an irony reminiscent of Anatole France, whom, by the way, Cabell had never read until he was accused of plagiarizing him.

More to the point, Jurgen held sexual intercourse. This diversion was described in terms of symbols so obvious that a contributor to Heywood Broun's column reported he had observed the book in the dressing-rooms of Broadway chorus girls. Cabell's contribution to early American sex literature lay not merely in his extraordinary frankness; he treated sexual diversion not as being necessarily reprehensible or admirable, but as being merely natural, which was an attitude so realistic that it remained for a professional enemy of realism to reduce it to print. And over the philanderings of Jurgen Cabell cast a radiance of poetry, wit, and what the young critics called 'civilized sophistication' which did a good deal to justify the conduct in parked cars and on country club lawns of young men who felt the same yearnings which Jurgen experienced when he beheld Dorothy and Helen and Anaïtis.

If the long legal ban on *Jurgen* denied Cabell the financial emoluments which are the just due of an author who writes well and the inevitable reward of an author who roams widely in the field of sex, whether he writes well or not, Cabell got his money on later books. *Figures of Earth*, *The Silver Stallion*, *The High Place*, and other books sold, if not as well as Harold Bell Wright's, then a good deal better than Miss Cather's; and Cabell became the object of a cult. In England Hugh Walpole rushed into print to proclaim of *Jurgen*, 'If America is looking for a book to show to Europe, here it is.' Cabell's popularity in England was so great that an English literary magazine produced an issue devoted entirely to him.

In America Mencken and Rascoe had the pleasure that belongs to the prophet as Wilson Follett in *The Dial*, John Macy, James Huneker, and other critics vied with each other in superlatives. *The Nation* saluted him as 'America's master ironist'; *The New Republic* admitted it was 'corrupted by Mr. Cabell's seductive prose'; and *The Bookman* added:

> The appearance in the field of American letters of James Branch Cabell is a phenomenon scarcely explicable. Here

is a writer who stands opposed to everything held holy by
the general reading public of today. There is no 'gladness'
in his books, no smug morality, no sodden sentiment. A
man could not be less a Puritan than Cabell. He has no
sweet and canting optimism, no deference to the Godly
Principle of Life as set down by Doctor Frank Crane. He
strives, not to shield illusions but destroy them, not to
glorify ideals but, mocking, laugh at them.

The younger generation admired him extravagantly: if
Fitzgerald was their god, then Cabell sat on his right side.
Familiarity with Cabell's bag of tricks — his word puzzles, his passages of poetry in prose, the elaborate historical 'sources' he invented for his supposedly medieval
tales, his symbolism — was almost as important on the
campus as bell-bottom trousers and a notebook containing
the telephone numbers of bootleggers. A group of young
men in Cleveland admired him so extravagantly they paid
to publish a book called *A Round-Table in Poictesme*, in
which they cried aloud in praise of their idol; and Warren
McNeill wrote a loving study of his prose called *Cabellian
Harmonics*.

Cabell had become a Personage. The Boston *Transcript*
and a few other journals sniped at him continually, but
for a few years he was regarded as the most eminent
literary man America had produced, and it was universally
conceded that if the works of any writer of the time lived,
they would be his. Cabell moved from the suburbs into a
large house on beautiful Monument Avenue in Richmond,
and gave teas at which was served a cocktail he invented
called the Ravished Virgin. Young men made pilgrimages
to see him, usually to be told over the telephone, no matter
what time they called, that Mr. Cabell was shaving. An

old scandal to the effect that he had killed a man was revived. In Richmond when he shopped for the little china animals which delight him he was regarded with awe.

FOLLOWERS OF THE LEADERS

LIKE Fitzgerald, Cabell had his imitators, and most of them were bad. The hull of his style could be copied, but the quality that gave it its magical beauty remained elusive, and a writer whom he influenced profoundly did not imitate the manner at all, but only his mocking, ironical, up-to-the-split-second modernity. He was Carl Van Vechten, and the book — not his first — was *The Blind Bow-Boy*. Van Vechten, like Cabell, made free use of the sex *motif*, but to Van Vechten the ancient way of a man with a maid was too prosaic: his theme was homosexuality. Van Vechten strove so hard and so conscientiously to be shocking that he became a little strained and silly. His heroine, Campaspe, scornful of her pathetically loving husband, is asked how she can tolerate his attentions to other women. '*Let* him, Fannie!' she replies. 'I encourage him!' A respectable old family is put in its bourgeoisie place with the remark, 'I'm sure they give turkey dinners Thanksgiving and Christmas.' Van Vechten catered to the selfish, egotistical younger generation with such remarks as 'We are the few. The rest are fools'; 'We both get what we want and we admire each other for it.' If what Van Vechten wanted was sales, a place in the literary sun, invitations to 'smart' and 'sophisticated' parties, he got them all.

Fitzgerald had an imitator in Dorothy Speare, Cabell in Van Vechten, and Sinclair Lewis had a horde of camp-followers. *Main Street* was the first of a library of books which mapped the American small town and exposed the spiritual poverty of the lives of its inhabitants. Most of the members of the Lewis school dealt solely with the Middle West, which soon took on in the American consciousness the combined characteristics of purgatory and the skeleton in the closet. E. Haldeman-Julius and his wife wrote the depressing *Dust* to show how a farm on the Kansas plains saps aspiration and enjoyment; the farm and the farmer both begin and end in dust, and the wife, broken by sorrow and labor, has to flee to a town to find peace. Ruth Suckow, an Iowan, informed us of the intolerable dullness of the small town; and Emanie Sachs, in *Talk*, a novel which her publishers made herculean efforts to get on the best-seller list, revealed that vicious village gossip can be more ruinous to a girl's life than a city slicker seducer. Sherwood Anderson, who began his career as a writer for Little Magazines, brought out another study of small-town life called *Poor White*. Zona Gale, after having it rejected as a serial by six magazine editors, got her fine *Miss Lulu Bett* published in book form to a critical acclaim which almost approached that aroused by *Main Street*.

YOUNGSTERS VIEW WITH CONTEMPT

THEODORE DREISER, silent for years after the censors pounced on *Sister Carrie*, began to sell again, and to be written about by grateful young men who had discovered he was carrying the banner of their revolt when they were in diapers. In 1920 *The Financier* was issued in Berlin by Kurt Wolff, *Twelve Men* in French by Rieder et Cie, and *Sister Carrie* by Les Éditions des Sirènes. Dreiser was old enough to be a Classic and sufficiently preoccupied with sex to be a Modern, and when it was said that in him America had a worthy candidate for the Nobel Prize, the Young Intellectuals pounded their typewriters in agreement.

For that was what they were now called.

The Young Intellectuals did not, of course, emerge suddenly and full-grown from the brow of H. L. Mencken. In their ranks were all the bright and sad young men and women who were giving distinction to the literary movement of the nineteen-twenties. What they needed was a tag. When England, which gave America the word 'panties,' invented 'Young Intellectuals,' the phrase united for the purposes of discussion the scattered, dissatisfied, and rebellious young people who were carrying on a guerrilla war against tradition and discipline. The phrase was at first used self-consciously and even a little shyly, but by 1922 it had been adopted with a belligerent, a chip-on-the-shoulder attitude by youthful malcontents who had broken into print and by their envious juniors on the campuses.

The Young Intellectuals did not all write books and articles. Some of them merely admired; but they were held in the loose bounds of the movement by a common distaste for the tradition and culture which they had inherited and which, since the war, had seemed inadequate, hypocritical, and silly. And most of the not-so-innocent bystanders intended, by and by, to write a masterpiece, when examinations were over or there was enough money to live on the Riviera; for this was a period in which a great fallacy descended upon the American people — the fallacy that anyone, given a typewriter, paper, and leisure, can write.

It was exciting to be a Young Intellectual. In the early nineteen-twenties the world of art and the mind seemed ineffably fresh to those who were becoming intellectually alive, and the world belonged to the young. Books that seemed more vital than books were ever to seem again were issuing from the presses of publishers who competed with each other for the productions of young men and women who had never had their names on title pages before. Geniuses were born overnight, and their quick fading from the scene went unnoticed in the excited flurry over the hordes of new geniuses who were forever arriving in New York. Literary reviews were devoured as speedily as newspapers, for 'discoveries' were being made with such frequency that merely keeping up with names, titles, and new startling points of view was almost a career.

If the public expression of the Young Intellectuals was

one of boredom and dissatisfaction, their contacts with each other were gay and sufficiently youthful to convince any Elder looking on that youth had not changed essentially. It was pleasant to drink gin at parties with literary young people and to assure each other that all laws were as absurd as the one which forced the host to mix his own gin of water and bootlegged alcohol. There was satisfaction in reflecting, over a Martini being shared with a bright young girl who had just downed hers in one gulp on a bet, that the generation which had adopted prohibition and had never heard of Freud was therefore incapable of running the world. One could make a hit by reading aloud such expressions of contempt as Harry Kemp's in *Tramping on Life* that 'the motto of the United States was not "Beauty is truth, truth beauty," but "Blessed be the man who can make two hills of corn grow where one bank of violets grew before,"' or Edith Sergeant's flaming injunction that one should not say at the end of a week, as one's grandmother did, 'What have I done to make others happy?' but 'What have I done that was amusing and exciting?'

How many writers and camp-followers enlisted under the crimson banner of the Young Intellectuals it is impossible to say. They had no fraternity pin, no initiation, no grip — though most of them were young enough to have escaped only recently from an adolescence in which those symbols of exclusiveness seemed important. Precise definition was likewise impossible, for the phrase — like 'realism' and 'romanticism' — had no meaning in a Noah Webster sense. The dates on birth certificates offered little assistance: Van Vechten was a Young Intellectual, but Hunter Stagg, who derisively called them the Y.I.'s in the Richmond *Reviewer*, denied strenuously that he was; Edmund Wilson, who was threatened with a spanking by an elder neighbor whom he had offended by an article in *The New Republic*, was, and Stuart Sherman, hardly a graybeard, was not. If the 'Intellectual' half of the tag meant that attitude was the criterion, how, a critic rose to ask, could Gilbert Seldes, John V. A. Weaver, and Joseph Wood Krutch, who unquestionably were Young Intellectuals, be classed together? The problem was a serious one for those who dealt with books in writing rather than in conversation, and the bewildered Burton Rascoe, having recovered from burns suffered when the false whiskers of a Santa Claus costume caught fire, returned to his typewriter to remark that four books by Young Intellectuals which he was disposing of in one review 'have not one point in common beyond the fact that they are made up of words from the English language, printed on paper, bound in covers, and written by men under thirty-five.'

But the quite natural desire for a pigeonhole led to various attempts at definition. Donald Ogden Stewart, whose parodies of current writers were a combination of wit, slapstick, and shrewd criticism, said in a speech: 'The younger generation has no morals. It has irony.' (Scott Fitzgerald in *The Beautiful and the Damned* said irony 'was the final polish of the shoe, the ultimate dab of the clothes-brush, a sort of intellectual There!') John V. A. Weaver offered the information that they read Conrad, not Wordsworth, because 'Wordsworth had forced the moral.' Doctor Henry Seidel Canby, a critic of sound scholarship who kept his balance during the turmoil of the decade, remarked that the younger novelists were romanticists who had grown up in an atmosphere of suspicion.

Not all the attempts at definition were friendly. Sherman incurred the everlasting hostility of the younger writers with a broadside in the *Atlantic Monthly* in which he defined a Young Intellectual (though he did not use the phrase) in a manner which started a controversy that lasted until Gertrude Atherton changed their name to 'Sophisticates' and thus confused the issue. To Sherman in his citadel at Urbana, Illinois, a Young Intellectual was a person who believed:

> That the twin incubi of Democracy and Puritanism have made beauty a prostitute to utility, and that the younger generation of artists and writers has seen through the solemn humbug of a future ideal republic, envisaging the failure of civilization not only in the present but in the future.
>
> That the younger generation desires only to be emancipated from the elder idealists, for it impo. .: its philosophy in fragments from beyond the borders of Anglo-Saxonia — from Ireland, Germany, France, and Italy, not forgetting to draw upon the quick Semitic intelligence.
>
> That art is 'letting oneself out completely and perfectly'; and that the chief thing to let out is the long repressed sexual impulses, recently unearthed by Sigmund Freud, for 'most of the evil in the world is due to self-control.'

For the Young Intellectuals Harold Stearns, a pugnacious young critic of American life, rose to denounce Sherman and to defend his contemporaries in an article in *The Bookman* called 'America and the Young Intellectual.'

> The problem [he wrote] is America *versus* the Young
> Intellectual.... And why, in the simplest sense of interest
> in intellectual things, should we hesitate to use the term?
> Why should it carry with it a faint aura of effeminate
> gentility?... The kernel of truth [in Sherman's attack], of
> course, is in the depiction of the younger generation as in
> revolt against the right-thinkers and the forward-lookers.
> It *is* in revolt; it *does* dislike, almost to the point of hatred
> and certainly to the point of contempt, the type of people
> who dominate in our present civilization, the people who
> actually 'run things.'...
>
> The Young Intellectual, the person not a genius yet
> with a certain competence and real interest in humanistic
> things ... will, perforce, be a part of the social and eco-
> nomic and educational machinery of the country, albeit it
> may be only a dissentient part. He will be interested in
> contemporary literature, in the type of university life we
> possess, in science, in art and the American theater, in the
> labor movement.

The seriousness of this manifesto, the official statement
of the movement by one of the several young men who
tried to push themselves into dominance, was reflected
in the declaration of Elizabeth Breuer to the feminine
wing: 'We must place all — even our womanliness —
into the jackpot. A soul is a bitter luxury. Are we young
women prepared to pay for one with love, family, and with
our social well-being, if need be?'

The movement, it will be seen, was quite serious, and
though Booth Tarkington, who wrote *Alice Adams* as an
'answer' to *Main Street*, told an interviewer he had never
heard of the Young Intellectuals, perceptive history will
record them as leading the only intellectual movement in
American history comparable to those movements which
lend excitement and variety to the intellectual develop-

ment of France. It was easy to ridicule them, and the
Elders did it with an infuriating effectiveness. Many
Y.I.'s were blatant, self-important, and egoistical. Many
were handicapped by a pale dilettantism, a willingness to
substitute facility and surface brilliance for the solid, hard
work which is always the lot of the artist and the thinker.
There was too often the annoyance of the spoiled child
that the world does not immediately recognize and reward
his unique talents. And there were such outcries as that
expressed by Stearns in his lecture to Sherman:

> Even the intelligent and tolerant desert us. Can we be
> blamed if we suspect that beneath the ostensible reasons
> lie others — fear, primarily, that an honest attempt to
> understand our point of view might make them deeply
> uncomfortable and dissatisfied? It is only a suspicion, but
> it is a growing one. Meanwhile, let Mr. Sherman reflect
> upon it while we of the younger generation make our plans
> for leaving the country of our birth and early affections.
> We do not want to cut ourselves off from our national life,
> but we are inexorably being forced to do it — many of us
> shall probably starve when we go to some alien country,
> but at least we shall be able, spiritually, to breathe.

II. BREATHING SPIRITUALLY

II. BREATHING SPIRITUALLY

We want works, straightforward, strong, accurate, and forever not understood.

TRISTAN TZARA: *A Manifesto*

THE deep spiritual breaths so necessary to the earnest Stearns were of no importance to the majority of young Paris-bound writers.

'I had supposed that any one . . . went to Paris because he liked to; because the wine is cheap, the girls pretty, the crêpes Suzette exalted, the Place de la Concorde beautiful,' said Sinclair Lewis, who went himself.

And, of course, because Paris is Paris and therefore the most glamorous and exciting city of all; because café-sitting is an invigorating sport; because one may carry a walking stick, wear a red and purple tie, and hear no snickering comment at all; because the steep streets of Montmartre nightly run with electric currents of gaiety.

In those hectic days you lived in a little apartment in Montmartre, or more respectably and expensively in Montparnasse; slept all day and played all night, or if you felt industrious, slept all day and wrote all night; knew there were gay and intelligent people to drink with and eccentric people to listen to; dropped around to the Dôme to hear the latest manifesto on the arts, delivered over a table with eight beer saucers on it by a very young expatriate who had once managed to sell a greeting-card verse for three dollars; threw your money (if you were one of the successes) around Paris of a soft spring evening until, buoyed by courtesy of Pernod Fils, you were sure few cafés in the city had not had the benefit of your riotous presence; went nonchalantly to *exhibitions* and homosexual and Lesbian dance-places so as to be able to pilot visiting Americans knowingly through the intricacies of Parisian sin.

And while you and your compatriots were enjoying yourselves as you never had before, American magazines and the Paris editions of the Chicago *Tribune* and the New York *Herald* were open forums to the expatriate question. Was it patriotic for Americans to live abroad? No! thundered the Babbitt millions back home. Americans belong in America; it is an American's duty to live in his country. Maybe it's not patriotic, returned the Young Intellectuals who were hoping to sail soon. But patriotism is hypocrisy, and America is a raw, bigoted country peopled with reformer fanatics. And the issue grew out of all proportion as stay-at-homes and travelers felt impelled to state in print their positions.

WHY THEY WENT

TYPICAL was the departure of Frank Ward O'Malley, former star of the New York *Sun*, for residence in Europe. O'Malley declared humorously but bitterly against all phases of American life. In long newspaper

AMERICANS IN PARIS
Expatriate magazines and revolutionary art manifestoes were
born over beer saucers on café tables

interviews he announced he was going away because of prohibition and increased drinking; because of the strangle-hold of organized gangster crime; because of the machinations of the Rotary Clubs; because the American population consisted chiefly of snoopers and tattle-tales; because of the imbecility and dishonesty of public officials; because of the poverty of *beaux arts;* because Americans were addicted to money-grubbing; because of the restlessness, hurry, and lack of leisurely enjoyment of what there was to enjoy; because the servants were ill-trained and overpaid; because, in spite of the efforts of chambers of commerce to convince him to the contrary, he considered the climate unsatisfactory.

Other writers stated less forceful reasons for taking passage east. Konrad Bercovici said he liked to play, that Parisians knew how and Americans (he excepted Sherwood Anderson) didn't. The first thing he did on arrival was to acquire a wine cellar. Ludwig Lewisohn maintained there was nothing finer than at the conclusion of a day's work to drop by the Dôme for a *café au lait*, settling the bill and *pourboire* for four and a half cents. Louis Bromfield announced that in Paris he could get a Better Perspective on American life. (This Better Perspective, very important in those days, was responsible for several grim and dusty farm life novels, conceived in Montparnasse and concerning the American Middle West.)

As for the people who came just because they wanted to, there were the Fitzgeralds, Scott and Zelda. After cutting a swath in New York after *This Side of Paradise*, the young author and his lovely wife burst on Paris. They dashed about in a Citroën, gave parties and were partied, and were altogether much gayer and less nostalgic than the undergraduates of whom Scott wrote. Hergesheimer wandered into the city frequently, just off on or just back from the far-flung travels he was always taking. Carl Van Vechten, scenting literary novelty, came to make his bows before Gertrude Stein, the portly sage of Rue de Fleurus. In fact all the literary big-wigs and little-wigs came at one time or another, if only for brief trips, and by 1922 Paris had become so hectic with visitors that some of the more hard-working expatriates fled to Rome in search of seclusion and quiet.

The most famous expatriate of them all was Ernest Hemingway, who became the college boy's idol and the fictional spokesman for the expatriates with *The Sun Also Rises*. After packing his left-over canned food in an army knapsack and carrying it around to Sherwood Anderson's apartment as a parting gift, he went to Paris as a press correspondent. His ensuing short stories in *In Our Time* and those printed in the *Transatlantic Review* and *This Quarter* made him known to the few, but *The Sun Also Rises* lifted him from the Young Intellectual class. It made him a Big Name. The young people particularly loved it; Dashiell Hammett had not yet written his detective novels, and it was the most drunken book to date. University of Virginia boys forgot their aloof pose and became enthusiastic enough to receive part of the credit for putting the book over. In Madrid American boys attempted to learn bullfighting, inspired by the Spanish *fiesta* scenes. Youngsters redoubled their efforts to make Father fork over sufficient cash for European trips, for they had learned from their new gospel that in Paris one could get drunk more often and more pleasantly and with nicer companions than anywhere in the world; that the Dôme, Rotonde, Select, Deux Magots, Napolitain, Dingo, and Zelli's were the places in which to drink; that charming, unmoral women like Lady Ashley (who was simultaneously in love with one man, about to marry another, and sleeping with her fiancé, with a bull-fighter, and with a Jew) might possibly be found in some of these bars and cafés.

So American youth, literary and otherwise, packed its typewriters and cocktail shakers and stormed Paris. When Ford Madox Ford, formerly Ford Madox Hueffer, started the *Transatlantic Review* there, this explanation of the place of publication was given in the prospectus:

> There is no young man, be his convictions what they may, who, if he has saved up but his railway fare and sixty centimes, will not fly to Paris and cry, '*Garçon, un bock!*' ... But the point is that they remain in Paris. You don't from here have to write to Oklahoma for contributions: from all the other proud cities you must.

But 'Ford's boys,' as were called those who rallied round his review, were of a more arty caliber than those collegians who responded to Hemingway's call. Their interests lay, far from the American-inspired Folies Bergères, in Sylvia Beach's Bookshop, where an open fire and comfortable chairs and discussion of James Joyce's *Ulysses* were sure to be found. Bobbed-haired Miss Beach made her Shakespeare and Company at No. 12 Rue de l'Odéon an intellectuals' rendezvous, a bookshop, a renting library, and a publishing house. Or Ford's boys might be interested in the Three Mountains Press, a publishing house started by William Bird, a Paris press correspondent who had always wanted to be a publisher. He bought a press and set up his 'house' on a quay of the Île St. Louis, and when Hemingway introduced Ezra Pound, Bird and Pound became shirt-sleeved and inky doing the printing themselves. It was a very esoteric sort of publishing; only first editions were printed, and these editions would total three hundred books per *opus*. In this way Bird brought out *Indiscretions* by Pound, *Women and Men* by Ford Madox Ford, *The Great American Novel* by W. C. Williams (a college mate of Pound's), and Hemingway's *In Our Time*. Another publisher was Robert McAlmon, who ran the Contact Publishing Company, business address at Miss Beach's; three hundred copies an edition and only one edition was his policy also. Miss Beach herself snapped up the best publishing morsel of the decade by bringing out *Ulysses*, the most idolized book on the Left Bank. Joyce was elevated to a more exalted position in literary Paris-America than were Cabell, Fitzgerald, and Lewis back home. Miss Beach undoubtedly hit upon a good thing, in prestige if not in cash.

EXILES TURN TO EDITING

FORD, of whom Mencken said, 'He has been the most promising young man in England for the past twenty years,' strove to make the *Transatlantic Review* influential, but his magazine was little heard of beyond the Left Bank.

Although he started with an imposing list of promised contributors his steadiest and most eminent was Hemingway. He finally folded the *Transatlantic Review* with a sigh of exhaustion — 'I had to edit it, put it to bed, see it packed in boxes, and delivered' — but he had the satisfaction of seeing it set the pattern for exile publications that followed. There were *Broom*, *Contact*, *Close Up*, *Tambour*. There was *The Little Review*, which emigrated to Paris from New York. *This Quarter*, run by Ethel Moorhead and Ernest Walsh, attracted literary insurgents for a while. Ezra Pound, who favored an editorial costume of velvet jacket and blue shirt, ordered the destiny of *Exile*.

All these periodicals called down the abuse of the schoolmen upon editors and contributors, but none so much as *transition* (it was enough for the academicians that the title was printed without capitals). 'Ravings of madmen,' 'dishonest quackery,' 'incredible imbecility,' 'neo-decadence,' 'anarchists,' 'the stuff of which nightmares are made,' were among the gentler criticisms it and its editors received. The latter were 'fanatic anti-Americans' too. *Life* printed a cartoon showing four drunken Americans in a Montparnasse bar, on their right hand a copy of *The Sun Also Rises* and on their left a copy of *transition*. One drunk is inquiring of the waiter, 'Garçon, what's that the orchestra's playing?' And the reply, 'Why, that's the Star-Spangled Banner, sir.'

A drastic 'revolution of the word' set off most of the ire against *transition* and created more consternation among readers and writers than anything since *The Little Review* went modern. Eugene Jolas, its editor, issued a manifesto to the effect that a large part of the existing vocabulary should be scrapped and the language should 'go towards a liberated expression' by substituting new words and new forms. (Jolas always explained his advanced-wing theories in the most precise and correct English.) Therefore he was quite willing to print Gertrude Stein, and Miss Beach lost the honor of again presenting James Joyce when *transition* ran serially *Work in Progress*, presenting 'the night-mind.' But *transition's* field was large and extended far beyond the cult of unintelligibility. It published English translations of the important work of the younger French, German, Soviet, and Spanish writers, and included Morley Callaghan, Hemingway, Kay Boyle, Robert M. Coates, Malcolm Cowley, Allen Tate, Hart Crane, Kathleen Cannell, John Herrmann, Samuel Putnam, Yvor Winters, William Carlos Williams, Alfred Kreymborg, Matthew Josephson, Whit Burnett, Harry Crosby, Stuart Gilbert, John Riordan, Katherine Ann Porter, Emily Holmes Coleman, Edgar Calmar, Waverly Lewis Root, Leigh Hoffman, Robert McAlmon, Horace Gregory.

During the few years *transition* was being published (the lives of exile magazines were always brief) it and its predecessors, contemporaries, and followers enjoyed Left Bank circulation and *entrée* to Greenwich Village and the homes of Young Intellectuals back in America. For they exemplified the spirit of experiment and revolt against tradition — played havoc with the established meanings of words, tried new arrangements of paragraphing and sentence structure — and a well-informed *révolté* had to keep up with their doings to make sure James Joyce and

Gertrude Stein had not become old-fashioned since the preceding issues.

The exile magazines, like the Little Magazines in America, were run in a genuinely non-commercial spirit. This was just as well — their appeal being to an extremely limited public, they rarely made money on circulation, and their advertising was almost non-existent. An editor was usually doubtful of the appearance of the next issue until it had come off the press. Printers frequently went unpaid for months. But for their brief spans the magazines managed to come out somehow, even if it was necessary to pass the hat at the Dôme. Few of them achieved *transition's* financial status. Jolas says, 'I gave up *transition* at a time when it threatened to become a mercantile success. It was being taken up by the snobs, the plagiarists, and the parasites.'

MISS STEIN IS IDOLIZED

THE snobs, plagiarists, and parasites had something else to take up when *transition* was done. Partly by that magazine's press-agenting of her, Gertrude Stein had become an institution. It was fashionable for bright young men to make pilgrimages from Iowa and Kansas to sit at her feet and listen to her flow of talk on this and that and 'art' and 'life' — talk which had the virtue of being far more lucid than her writings. But the baffling thing to Miss Stein's bitterest critics was her capacity for exciting the admiration of America's most worth-while writers, aside from that of the esthetes. Sherwood Anderson, Van Vechten, Fitzgerald, and Hemingway came and chatted, listened and went away to broadcast highest praise. 'She may be, just *may* be, the greatest word-slinger of our generation,' offered Anderson. It is possible to find passages in *A Farewell to Arms* and in Fitzgerald's books that thrill with their vague loveliness and startle by their evident kinship with Miss Stein's theories. Van Vechten dogged her footsteps faithfully as she toured America in the winter of 1935 making lectures in her famous 'rose is a rose is a rose' style.

Gertrude Stein was born in 1872 in Allegheny, Pennsylvania, migrated at the age of one to Vienna and Paris, then returned to live in California. While at Radcliffe College she was tremendously impressed by Louisa M. Alcott and William James. At Johns Hopkins she surprised her professors with her progress in brain anatomy, but became bored with their entreaties that she realize her ability and do more work. She threw down medicine, and 1903 found her in Paris in the early stages of her incarnation as literary prophet and judge. *Three Lives* was her first book; the indifference of publishers caused her to 'pay her own admission' by publishing it herself. *The Making of Americans*, in its final incarnation seven and one half inches wide, nine and one half inches long, and four and one half inches thick, accumulated dust for nearly twenty years before an enthusiastic friend prodded a publisher into printing it. ('I am working for what will endure, not for a public,' said Miss Stein at one time.)

But by 1926, publication of anything of Miss Stein's was a smart move. She was now a vogue. People were frequenting her salon, coming to hear her talk, to view her collection of the work of Picasso, Braque, Juan Gris, Matisse, sitting on the heavy, straight-backed chairs and scanning the crowd for these artists who were her intimate friends, watching the self-effacing dark little Alice B. Toklas, Miss Stein's secretary who later became famous when Miss Stein wrote her autobiography, which was really the autobiography of Miss Stein.

The critics could no longer ignore Miss Stein as they had for twenty years. She was being published and written about and talked about. So they read her back home and critical hackles rose in anger. 'If this is literature or anything other than stupidity worse than madness, then has all criticism since the beginning of letters been mere idle theorizing,' stormed Doctor Henry Seidel Canby's *Saturday Review of Literature;* and echoes rose from other alarmed sentries of criticism. Miss Stein had suddenly become such a force that it seemed necessary to lambaste her critically far harder and at greater length than her importance deserved. If this was not done, it was rumored and feared, single-handed she would overthrow the language and set up some weird new babbling in its place. And on the pro-Stein side of the argument Jean Cocteau wrote: 'I can sense her rhythm even in translation; she possesses the *métier poétique*. Her *Portrait of Picasso* is like a bas-relief; I seem to run my fingers over it, as though it were a piece of plastic art. Hers was the first writing which struck me as being a new thing in the English language.' In the same breath with her work were mentioned *Kubla Khan* and *Ulalume*.

While battles were being waged over her short-cropped gray head it is safe to say no one knew what her writing meant. 'A Patriotic Leading' from *Useful Knowledge* needs revelation to explain it. It goes:

Verse 1

    Indeed indeed.

    Can you see.

    The stars

    And regularly the precious treasure.

    What do we love without measure.

    We know.

Verse 2

    We suspect the second man.

Verse 3

    We are worthy of everything that happens.

    You mean weddings.

    Naturally I mean weddings

Verse 4

    And there we are.

    Hail to the nation.

Verse 5

    Do you think we believe it.

Verse 6

    It is that or bust.

Verse 7

    We cannot bust.

Verse 8

    Thank you.

Verse 9

    Thank you so much.

Miss Stein has said, 'All this foolishness about my writing being mystic or impressionistic is so stupid. Just a lot of rot. I write as pure, straight, grammatical English as anyone, more **accurate** grammatically than most.... Everything I write means exactly what it says.'

Miss Stein was responsible for a minor tragedy in *transition*. The harassed French printers managed to get in all her words but set them in the wrong order (it is not known who caught the error). The piece announces that if you halve a river and harbor you have a river and harbor, and concludes indecisively with:

> I think I won't
> I think I will
> I think I will
> I think I won't
> I think I won't
> I think I will
> I think I will
> I think I won't

Although such writing was hooted, blasted, and cursed, Miss Stein's followers made capital out of critical animosity. They enjoyed attacks on her with much the same glee with which Mencken received the news he was a 'putrid public pest.' Her influence increased and her pronunciamentoes were regarded with awe and reverence. She was a typical literary idol of the 'twenties, when the style in idols leaned toward the spectacular. And so she rode triumphantly through the decade and a little into the 'thirties, when the American Medical Association took note of the fact that a person whose literary motto is 'a rose is a rose is a rose' must be afflicted with a type of insanity called echolalia. The lecture tour finally broke the myth that Stein is wonderful if you can understand her; audiences were alternately bored and amused, and left knowing that hereafter they could laugh at a remark like 'toasted Suzy is my ice-cream' without feeling uncomfortably lacking in culture. The knockout blow came March 1, 1935, when her old friends of the Paris colony, having read her *Autobiography of Alice B. Toklas*, issued a pamphlet called *Testimony Against Gertrude Stein*. In this Henri Matisse writes, 'Miss Stein has contacted indiscriminately things about which... she has understood nothing.' 'For one who poses as an authority on the epoch it is safe to say she never went beyond the stage of the tourist,' says George Braque. André Salmon, critic: 'What confusion! What incomprehension of an epoch!' and Eugene Jolas concludes, 'Hollow, tinsel bohemianism and egocentric deformations.'

And so Miss Stein, after her happy success, was laid away in moth balls; in all probability the only further reference that will be made to her is as a monumental literary curiosity of the nineteen-twenties.

BROTHERHOOD OF THE HOBBYHORSE

THE decade that could bring a Stein to full flower could do far more fantastic things, could make a French word meaning 'hobbyhorse' a synonym for the most advanced wing of art. The Dadaists set out to outdo Futurism, Cubism, Vorticism as much as those isms had outdone Impressionism. The movement received more publicity than all its predecessors put together; by virtue of this publicity and the enterprise of its adherents it became the sensation of the artistic world by the early 'twenties.

The Dada label is accounted for in various ways. Tristan Tzara, a Roumanian Jew whose authentic name nobody seems ever to have heard, gives a grandiloquent explanation: 'In Switzerland I was in the company of friends and was hunting the dictionary for a word appropriate to the sonorities of all languages. Night was upon us when a green hand placed its ugliness on the page of Larousse, pointing very precisely to "dada." My choice was made.' Less dramatic but more plausible is the version holding that a group composed of Wielande, Herzfelde (famous as the author of the phrase 'Every man his own football'), Tzara, Ball, Janko, and Arp used to meet for discussion in a Zurich cabaret where one Mlle. Dada sang. Enjoying her voice over beer and esthetics, they named their movement for her. Incidentally the fact of Dada's inception in Zurich is considered significant by Dadaists, for at the time this occurred Lenin and Joyce were in the city, the latter working on *Ulysses*.

The dust of the rumpus kicked up by Dada's prancings is now cleared away, but more than that is necessary for the elucidation of its theories. The movement was regarded as a wholesome tonic against the academicians, as 'the destroyer of the gods of buncombe.' One almost-Dadaist, Sheldon Cheney, saw the object of the movement as purposelessness and continued to say, quite seriously, that Dadaists go beyond other iconoclasts by destroying iconoclasm 'and when that is destroyed, Dada will destroy Dada, hell will be plumbed, and then light again.'

It is inconceivable in these comparatively rational

'thirties that people could become upset over anything so inane, that they should so tremblingly receive the menacing Dadaist manifestoes. But the ultra-conservatives lost their heads completely; one blessedly anonymous critic shiveringly saw Dada as a 'universally inclusive, desperately serious, supremely conscious hoax intended to undermine the whole fabric of decadent European society.' It was to accomplish this by knocking out one at a time the props of art, culture, and religion.

Their methods for ruining the world were vague. The first move in this direction was to give the title of president to every member of the group (one Dadaist referred to himself as President of the World). The issuance of manifestoes, usually unintelligible and funny enough to be widely repeated, at international meetings in Paris was another of their subversive activities. It wasn't essential to do this in Paris or at a meeting; manifestoes could be pronounced anywhere at any time. Dadaists were a gregarious lot, however, and assemblies were popular, particularly the ones at which a speaker put his voice in hopeless competition against the continuous clanging of an electric bell. They did work occasionally, however, just enough to keep the academicians and the public in a dither of irritation and laughter.

Francis Picabia, who competed with Tzara for the place of chief Dadaist, displayed his pictures full of beautifully round circles, resembling depiction of the inside of a watch by means of a compass. More popular Dadaist painting was that of the type done by Georg Grosz, very juvenile and sketchy; his Murder, which looks as though James Thurber might have rendered it in his childhood,

SERPENT

SORROW
AND
"THE FALL"

RADIANCE

MOTHER
EARTH

'EVE' AND 'GOD ALONE'
Brancusi and Sever go through some Dadaist convolutions

was called by a brother Dadaist 'a stark and moving thing.' There was the composition of other sorts of masterpieces, such as the one consisting of single words clipped from papers and magazines placed in a glass case in the company of an eye-dropper, one bean, one stamp, pieces of string, and a pocket compass.

Their dramatic attempts were particularly interesting; two accredited Dadaists wrote a play in which the leading characters were an umbrella, a sewing machine, and a bathrobe. But it was in the field of poetry that they really hit their stride. Take, for instance, 'Suicide' by Louis Aragon:

$$A \ b \ c \ d \ e \ f$$
$$g \ h \ i \ k \ l$$
$$m \ n \ o \ p \ q \ r$$
$$s \ t \ u \ v \ w$$
$$x \ y \ z$$

This, of course, would have been quite inartistic if Aragon had admitted the letter j.

Big-Shot Tzara, of whom it was said, 'His sincerity is such that he dumps his personality in front of the world without reserve or arrangement... and his style is strictly adequate,' achieved this:

> a e ou a youyouyou i e ou o
> youyouyou
> drrrrrdrrrrrdrrrrrgrrrrrrgrrrrrgrrrrrrrr
> bits of green duration flutter
> in my room
> a e o i ii ea ou ii ii belly
> shows the center I want to take it
> ambran bran bran and restore
> center of the four
> beng bong beng bang...

Many of the intellectuals, American and Paris-American, were interested in the Dadaists and partly accepted their theories of art. But few were willing to go the whole hog and admit, 'I am a Dadaist.' One such was Matthew Josephson, one of the distressingly small number of the group to grow up. Josephson was in the Columbia crowd that included Lewis Mumford.

After college he took the magazine *Broom* on its long travels, acting as editor in Rome, Paris, and New York, and tending its death-bed in the latter city. He was an assistant editor on *transition* in the company of Robert Sage, Stuart Gilbert, and Harry Crosby. All this was fine enough, but Josephson definitely sloughed off Dadaism with the publication of *Zola and His Time* and a biography of Jean Jacques Rousseau — both showing far more astute critical judgment than could be demonstrated by any Dadaist, and being much too competently written for any follower of that airily ununderstandable cult.

This, then, was literary Paris-America of the 'twenties. A Paris swarming with young Americans 'living their own lives.' A Paris where reigned Gertrude Stein, a Pennsylvania girl who grew hefty and made good. A Paris full of Dadaists solemnly concocting their puerile tricks. It was a time and a place filled with fun and revolt and intensity and wine. And it all blew up like a bubble when the bottom fell out of the American stock market.

It was slated for an early death, anyway. The expatriates had grown a little older and perhaps a little less gay, and to remain in Paris was like being the old grad who comes back to too many class reunions. The number of marriages and resultant lapses into domesticity were disconcertingly many. The Dadaists had run out of amusing tricks, and Gertrude Stein didn't seem as thrillingly modern as she used to. The drinks were as good and the Paris nights as soft and sweet, but the kick had gone out of things.

III. CENSORSHIP: FROM LIMBS TO LEGS

III. CENSORSHIP:
FROM LIMBS TO LEGS

I would rather a child of mine take opium than read one of
those books. . . . There cannot be viler language, there
cannot be words put together so vile and rotten as in those
books. . . . I want to keep them all out. I would rather keep
out a thousand, than have one mistake made.

REED SMOOT of Utah, on the floor of the U.S. Senate

IN KNOXVILLE, Tennessee, word got around that a
play called *Rain* was coming to town. Miss Mary Boyce
Temple, head of the local United Daughters of the Con-
federacy, although she had neither seen the play, read it
nor Somerset Maugham's short story — in fact had *Rain*
confused with Elinor Glyn's *Three Weeks* — gave this
statement to the press:

> We do not fear the effect which such a play would have
> on us. We of the D.A.R. and the United Daughters of the
> Confederacy have had the advantages of education and
> travel and have been prepared for such things. Such a
> play would not injure us; it would only disgust us.
> But there are other women who have not had these
> advantages, and there are the young people who are inex-
> perienced in the problems of life. It is for their benefit and
> protection that we seek to prevent the showing of such
> plays in Knoxville.
> Such a play would not injure me, but I have seen the
> world. Nobody knows the world better than I. No woman

has had greater educational advantages, has been more in
social life, or has traveled more than I. I am able to judge
of the temptations that come to the young and inexperienced. It is the duty of us to protect those who have not
had our advantages.

On the strength of this statement *The Nation* and
Joseph Wood Krutch nominated this Knoxville Daughter
the perfect censor. All the characteristics were there —
self-importance, desire for publicity, large display of
virtue, vagueness of expression, and intention 'to protect
those who have not had our advantages,' that is, to keep
others from enjoyment.

The amateur censor's mind was surely a strange ag-
glomeration of false ideals, topped by an astounding willingness to busy itself noisily for no remuneration. John S.
Sumner, secretary of the New York Society for the Suppression of Vice, and the Reverend J. Frank Chase, holding
the same position in the Watch and Ward Society of
Boston, received adequate salaries for their work, but
Miss Temple could have got little for her pains but
promotion at the next D.A.R. election. Nevertheless, the
'twenties brought to light numbers of such selfless persons
eager to expound the viciousness of various books, plays,
and magazines they had not read (but in most cases would
read shortly), and when they made dark mention of what
these books, plays, and magazines would do to 'the young
people who are inexperienced in the problems of life,' they
found a large and receptive audience. This audience,
worrying over their children, temporarily overlooked the
arguments of Milton and forgot that this 'questionable'
literature was too adult to interest their offspring —

who for the large part were confining their reading to the confession magazines which specialize in the inducement of sexual excitement.

MORE FALLACIES AND FOOLISHNESS

THE entire fabric of censorship, professional and otherwise, was riddled with fallacies and absurdities. The initial fallacy lay in the belief that suppression of a book kept people from reading it. This was so far from true that many books which otherwise would have commanded little attention and sale reaped long notices and profits from censorship. When complaint of a book was made, papers printed the news, and before the suppression became effective it was selling to a now alert public with redoubled speed. Copies were exhausted, prices soared, and 'booklegging' became immensely profitable. The public, having been told it must not read a book, tracked down copies with diligence and did not flinch at fifty-dollar prices. Before the excitement died the publisher quickly issued new editions of the author's past endeavors which, as in the case of Cabell's works after the suppression of *Jurgen*, sold in far greater quantities than had the first printings. Magazine editors, impressed by the notoriety, would pay top prices for stories they had previously rejected. Far from disgracing and impoverishing author and publisher, censorship brought them velvet.

The blacklists of the Watch and Ward Society, the Society for the Suppression of Vice, the Post Office Department, the United States Customs, and public libraries seldom agreed as to what was 'obscene, lewd, lascivious, filthy, indecent, and disgusting,' so that even in Boston, the strongest fort of censorship in America, it was possible to receive through the mails books forbidden in the city. There was always some way to procure a banned book, no matter in what section of heavily censored America one happened to be. Occasionally censors snatched a book that had been out for two or three years, suddenly discovering it a menace to youth. Young people had already read and forgotten it, and the action brought new publicity to a book whose sales had died.

Library boards were guilty of excesses of foolishness. One committee of readers, who felt themselves quite sophisticated, enjoyed Aldous Huxley, but thought *Antic Hay* and *Crome Yellow* too rough for their clientèle, so did not purchase library copies. When *Two or Three Graces* was published they refused it admission to their shelves, not because it was immoral but because it was not up to *Antic Hay* and *Crome Yellow*. In the reform school of Minneapolis juvenile delinquents were denied the *Saturday Evening Post*, *Red Book*, and the *Ladies' Home Journal*. A Socialist alderman considered the first disrespectful to labor unions, a conservative alderman claimed *Red Book* glorified criminals; a labor leader said the *Ladies' Home Journal* was namby-pamby and therefore a bad influence. Being unable to agree, they upheld each other, and the boys and girls were denied the most innocuous of current literature.

The biggest stumbling-block to the cause of censorship was the word 'obscene.' Obscenity, quite obviously, is a subjective thing, varying from person to person. Much of what is filthy to John Sumner is fine literature to Heywood Broun — as both these gentlemen have lost no opportunity to mention. Obscene literature is illegal, but what constitutes obscene literature, outside the field of obvious pornography, it is impossible to say. As Stuart Sherman observed, under the liquor laws the presence of alcohol was sought in the liquor, but under obscenity laws the presence of obscenity was not sought in the book but in the minds of the juries. Sherman reduced the argument of censorship to abject absurdity by commenting that a jury sitting in judgment on a book must 'conjecture whether a book is indecent by first conjecturing how it will affect young minds which are, conjecturally, open to the conjecturable influences of such a book.'

Censorship, in spite of the gaping holes in its argument, was much in the air, owing chiefly to the wave of sexiness that in the 'twenties affected manners and flooded over into literature. Conservatives grew jittery when they observed what a bold hussy literature had become. Pope Pius was alarmed at those books which hide lewdness 'under a cloak of false religious mysticism.' Professor Bliss Perry of Harvard said, 'The American public is now facing a clear and present danger through unclean books.' The Charleston *News and Courier* announced that no one 'can doubt that the flood of nastiness in books is really one of the gravest problems of these times, and no decent man or woman ... is going to try to hinder any worthwhile effort to solve that problem in so far as it can be solved.'

The Richmond *News Leader* was indignant over the 'scores of young authors in America who are writing neither literature nor science, but naked ugly filth ... solely because it gets them an audience (such as it is) they cannot procure by an honorable effort.' And the Newark *Times* said the 'fair orgies of sensuality' were positively 'dizzying' as far as it was concerned. Die-hard Hamlin Garland became more analytical with

> Several of our younger novelists are bringing to our fiction that eroticism which has so long been the peculiar province of 'the French novel.' In others the brutal plainness of speech of certain Scandinavian writers and the pessimistic animalism of modern Russian novelists appear, while many of the English novels imported by our publishers are of the decadent quality of Matisse and Archepenko. ... I believe in censorship.

BATTLING SALACITY

AND so the censors, encouraged, bent to their labors. In the Port of New York the Mardrus-Mather translation of *The Arabian Nights*, an expensive edition intended for scholars, was held by customs men because it was unexpurgated. Hergesheimer's home town of West Chester, Pennsylvania, considered his *Cytherea* too shocking to be admitted into its public library. Canada, bitten by its neighbor's vice bug, barred the New York *Daily Mirror* as 'immoral.' As the Peaches Browning case showed signs of going in too heavily for perversion the Camden *Courier* and other newspapers declined to print further testimony, confining their reports to short summaries.

New York Supreme Court Justice John Ford found his daughter reading D. H. Lawrence's *Women in Love* and hurriedly called a meeting to which came representatives of religious and social organizations. The Clean Book League was formed, with its object to make the law against obscene books 'horse-high, pig-tight and bullstrong' (a fair sample of censorship phraseology). Ford got a bill, the Cotillo-Jesse Clean Book Bill, before the New York State Senate, and when it was defeated announced he was going to use other modes of attack against the 'saturnalia of obscenity.'

When Bronson Cutting, Senator from New Mexico, proposed the deletion from the Tariff Act of the provision against obscene books, Senator Smoot from Ute (as Ogden Nash has called Reed Smoot) lugged onto the Senate floor for the purpose of exhibition an armful of what he considered sinful books and announced, 'If a customs inspector at the Port of New York, with his knowledge of the world, regards on his own initiative a book as obscene, it is about the nearest approach to jury trial that can be had.'

Customs inspectors, he continued, are 'men of education, legal training, and broad information,' and therefore Senator Cutting's plan was ridiculous, as it provided for leaving questions of literary obscenity to the federal and state clean books laws, thereby depriving customs men of the privilege of lifting from the luggage of annoyed travel-

ers any books they might want to read. The Senator
spluttered and stormed that ten minutes spent on Joyce's
Ulysses is 'enough to indicate that it is written by a man
with a diseased mind and soul so black that he would even
obscure the darkness of hell. Nobody would write a book
like that unless his heart was just as rotten and as black as
it could possibly be.'

Smoot made himself increasingly ridiculous and Cutting
won his spurs from the intellectuals as the fight went on, to
end finally in a compromise (really a victory for Cutting)
which provided that books considered obscene by customs
inspectors were to be held by the collector of the port until
the nearest district court had time to give judgment.

The censorship bug bit others than vice-snoopers. In
Sacramento a patriotic society attempted to amend
American history on the ground that the initiative, refer-
endum, recall, and direct primary are un-American. Los
Angeles banned *The Nation* and *The New Republic* from
its schools. Liberal Wisconsin barred histories which did
not treat the founding fathers with proper reverence.
San José, California, did not permit textbooks too favorable to England — only a few years before, fair treatment
of Germany had been unpatriotic. All over the country
Darwin, Huxley, Spencer, Marx, Wells, and Van Loon
were making difficulties for college trustees.

IN DEFENSE OF FREE SPEECH

IN THE meantime, an immensely articulate group banded for the purpose of fighting censorship, which appeared an ever-increasing encroachment upon personal liberty. Authors and critics shouted loudest and most effectively against the bugaboo, but they had the support of many other intelligent Americans who were appalled at the restrictions being laid upon their private lives in what was advertised as the freest country in the world. A continual barrage of derision, with heavy cannon brought up with each new action for suppression, was aimed at the institution of censorship and the vice societies which fostered it. The supposed supporters of censorship, the Y.M.C.A., mothers' clubs, Boy Scouts, Camp Fire Girls, and such organizations came in for a large share of critical lambasting. Tactics were varied. Gentle fun was an accepted method, as was impartial criticism, but rowdy jeers were more in vogue. Occasionally defenders of the Bill of Rights resorted to language as extreme as that employed by the vice societies in their prosecutions. Censors were labeled 'illiterate,' 'blackmailing,' 'filthy-minded,' 'impertinent,' 'meddlesome,' 'fanatical.'

Literary big-wigs were hot against the Sumners of the 'twenties, and no opportunity was overlooked to make that clear. Among the kinder remarks on censorship: Broun — 'There is a distinct affinity between fools and censorship'; Sherwood Anderson — 'The whole notion of

censorship is absurd'; Fitzgerald — 'The clean book bill
will be one of the most immoral measures ever adopted ...
they'll attack Hergesheimer, Dreiser, Anderson, and Cabell, whom they detest because they can't understand';
Mencken — 'In the long run the advocates of comstockery
are bound to win. This is a moral republic, and the spirit
of its laws is obviously against the free interchange of
ideas. Meanwhile I see no reason for alarm. No matter
what laws are passed, it will always be possible to evade
them'; Joseph Wood Krutch — 'Censors may be drawn
from many classes — from the stupid, the humorless, the
fanatical, and the prurient — but one class from which
they cannot be drawn is the class of decent and intelligent
men'; Cabell said circumstances 'beyond, as the phrase is,
my control' made him too biased to comment, but the
revised edition of *The Cream of the Jest* reveals his amused
bitterness on the matter.

Vociferous collaborators came out with *Nonsenseorship*,
an agile affair which hit hard at the censors but impartially
spread denunciation over most of the phenomena of
American civilization. Broun, Ruth Hale, George S.
Chappell, Ben Hecht, Wallace Irwin, Frederick O'Brien,
Dorothy Parker, John V. A. Weaver, Charles Hanson
Towne, Robert Keable, Helen Bullitt Lowry, Frank
Swinnerton, H. M. Tomlinson, Alexander Woollcott, and
the author of *Mirrors of Washington* were contributors, and
many of them helped form the Committee for the Suppression of Irresponsible Censorship, the avowed purpose
of which was 'to combat the insistent activities of the
descendants of Anthony Comstock.'

The diverse talents and viewpoints represented give a

clear idea of the prevalence of an enthusiasm for censor-sniping in literary circles. Jim Tully, Rex Beach, Hergesheimer, Edwin Björkman, Floyd Dell, Fannie Hurst, Edgar Lee Masters, Mary Roberts Rinehart, William Allen White, Hendrik Van Loon, Ernest Boyd, Robert W. Chambers, Lee Wilson Dodd, Ernest Poole, Amelie Rives Troubetskoy were a few of those who banded 'to call attention to the dangers from bigotry and blind prejudice that threaten to stifle the intellectual life of the country.'

There were many literary people who did not agree with the aims of this organization, that pornography laws should be enforced only against pornography, recognizable as such, and panaceas of all sorts were prescribed throughout the pages of current magazines. Sherman felt that since the passing of the scholars and gentlemen who used to produce American letters the distinction between art and erotica had been wiped away; therefore the only solution was a dispassionate criticism of doubtful books, with the critics to possess a 'conception of public welfare that includes the interests of both literature and morality.' Henry Seidel Canby believed in enforcement of pornography laws, but would leave to public opinion judgment of books of merit which contain lurid passages, and would educate public opinion away from squeamishness. Brander Matthews considered censorship a province for the police only. George Barr McCutcheon thought the writer should be his own censor and 'study the difference between liberty and license.'

Sumner himself offered an idea: that publishers doubtful about a manuscript should submit it to a jury of twelve, drawn from a panel of five hundred representative citizens.

These would not be professional snoopers, as they are 'likely to fall into a rut and begin to lay down rules such as forbidding the description of a woman's legs or of a passionate kiss.' This proposal received universal boos; the National Association of Book Publishers called it 'preposterous' and announced it was the last so-called solution to the problem they would consider. Heywood Broun offered the only truly gay plan:

> If we should choose our censors from fallible folk we might have proof instead of opinions. Suppose the censor of *Jurgen* had been someone other than Mr. Sumner, someone so unlike the head of the vice society that after reading Mr. Cabell's book he had come out of his room, not quivering with rage, but leering and wearing vine leaves. In such case the rest would be easy. It would merely be necessary to shadow the censor until he met his first dryad. His wink would be sufficient evidence and might serve as a cue for the rescuers to rush forward and save him. Of course there would then be no necessity for legal proceedings in regard to the book. Expert testimony as to its possible effects would be irrelevant. We should know, and we could all join cheerfully in the bonfire.

Few living persons can remember an uncensored America. Prior to 1873 the reading of fragile womanhood and the Negro population had been carefully selected, but white males were free to read what they chose. The mails were not closed to so-called obscene matter, the press printed advertisements of contraceptives, and it is significant that there were fewer of the dirty postcards, confession and art magazines, and smutty joke books that infested the censored era inaugurated by Anthony Comstock. When this fighting fanatic came into power, got the Comstock Act (Penal Section 1141) on the books, and whipped into shape the New York Society for the Suppression of Vice, suppression closed down on the country — on America which had forgotten that forty years before, Clay, Calhoun, and Webster on the Senate floor had declared censorship of the mails an unconstitutional and risky business, and which ignored the fact that censorship's sponsor was a man of so chilling a temperament as to pass the time estimating the number of railroad box cars it would take to hold the men he had sent to jail.

The age of gentility welcomed rather than resented what George Bernard Shaw named 'comstockery.' It was, as has been so often remarked, a prudish era, and the invasion of private rights seemed a small price to pay to down the hellish phenomena described by Comstock. Censorship was not an issue but a gratefully received protection, and there were few voices, literary or otherwise, raised against it. Writers and critics were well-bred in those days — Sherman's wistfully remembered scholars and gentlemen who were more interested 'in the life of the mind than the life of the senses.'

SUMNER, HEIR TO COMSTOCK

THEN the 'twenties hove into view. Literary people forgot correct deportment, and suddenly censorship was an issue, to be protested, battled, and cursed. The heartiest damning issued from New York, where lived most of the writers of the country, and the natural target was Sumner and his vice society. This tight-lipped expert on obscenity made but little dent on the consciousness of New York until he banned Cabell's *Jurgen* and received such abuse for it that probably only his stern Christian sense of duty prevented him from wishing he had refrained. For the absence of *Jurgen* from bookshops made the *literati* fighting mad, and they determined to break the power of the vice society by concentrating their forces on the one case instead of delivering futile and scattered volleys at the system.

During *Jurgen's* long incarceration — over two years — while booksellers were profiting truly magnificent sums on the surreptitious sale of the few copies left extant, the new generation of American letters was exerting its suddenly acquired influence in proclaiming *Jurgen* a most lovely work and the vice society a most unlovely organization and the principle of literary censorship as vicious a thing as ever concocted by a reformer. An 'emergency committee' organized to fight for the book and the public soon received from it a detailed report on the case, *Jurgen and the Censor*. When the case finally came into the Court of General Sessions it was seen that the publishers, McBride, had employed brilliant counsel, and Garrard Glenn made what is considered a classic attack on the censorship of books.

The battle had been worth the time, money, and indignation spent on it, for Judge Nott advised acquittal with 'In my opinion the book is one of unusual literary merit and contains nothing "obscene, lewd, lascivious, filthy, indecent or disgusting" within the meaning of the statute and the decisions of the courts of the state in similar cases.' Cabell wrote his satiric *Taboo*, brought out in a very limited edition, and all around writers gladly greeted a new era wherein the vice society would have little part.

They underestimated Sumner's tenacity, earnestness, and sincerity. They overlooked the fact that the statute provided that copies of a book must be seized upon complaint, a warrant for the arrest of the publisher issued, and sale stopped until three judges of Special Sessions or a twelve-man jury in General Sessions agreed with the complaint, when the book was suppressed for good, or until the courts decided on release. Even if Sumner could not get the judges to agree with him on the salaciousness of a book, he could temporarily put out of circulation one he deemed unfit for the public's tender eyes. He also could engage in oral and written bouts with the anti-censors and thus keep his cause well before the public, so that John D. Rockefeller, Jr., Thomas A. Edison, the Colgate soap family, and other influential persons would continue their support of the organization which gave him a job.

His arguments with Broun, one of which was conducted through *The Bookman*, made evident the intellectual gulf between the opposing camps. The two viewpoints were so far apart that Broun and Sumner hardly came within sniping distance of each other, a fact accentuated by Sumner's inability to express himself with clarity and directness and to remain within the confines of the subject. His 'answer' was chiefly employed to make it plain he was not a censor: 'We know of no censorship of literature in

this country. We know of no functionary having authority to review books prior to publication and prohibit the
publication of those which in his opinion ought not to be
published.' And in hurt phrases he insisted Broun had no
love for the society (a correct assumption) and therefore
called it an organization of censors, as the word had an
unpleasant connotation to the public mind.

The disparity in the ideas of these men, representative
of their respective groups, was such that Sumner wondered in print who Broun represented in making this 'plea
for obscene literature,' when the latter had merely said, 'I
personally believe there ought to be a certain amount of
what we now know as immoral writing.' For the man who,
in regard to *Jurgen* said, 'The greater the artist, the more
important to suppress him when he traverses the conventional standards,' to hold a public debate with Ernest
Boyd, to whom moralistic literature was anathema, was a
fruitless enterprise. Nevertheless, the debate took place
and was entertaining if not instructive. The critic said
obscenity could not be defined and Sumner replied that it
could. Sumner again maintained he was no censor and
further stated, 'I don't claim to know anything about
literature.' And this, aside from a few politely unpleasant
remarks about each other, was the upshot of the matter.

Sumner continued to wage his war as energetically
though not as picturesquely as Comstock had. Having
downed *Jurgen* temporarily, he turned on the *Satyricon* of
Petronius, the anonymous *A Young Girl's Diary*, Arthur
Schnitzler's *Casanova's Homecoming*, Radclyffe Hall's *The
Well of Loneliness*, Théophile Gautier's *Mademoiselle de
Maupin*, the anonymous *Madeleine*, an autobiography of a

prostitute, Maxwell Bodenheim's *Replenishing Jessica*, and, at the instigation of Justice Ford, Lawrence's *Women in Love*.

In 1925 Sumner was able to announce that for the past six years he had obtained four hundred and seventy-five arrests. His yearly report looked splendid, but the fact remained that, although he could tuck books away for a short time, he was powerless to keep them from the public permanently. Judges were showing a disconcerting tendency to remove one by one the longest teeth of the Comstock Act. All the above-mentioned books were eventually released, and with each acquittal a little of the efficacy of the censorship law was whittled away, this in spite of Sumner's feverish lobbying to preserve the act in its 1873 status.

By 1930 he found himself in the embarrassing position of being forced to admit that during the decade he had not been able to suppress any book issued by a reputable publisher through the usual channels and considered by reputable critics to possess any literary merit. There had been plenty of arrests and fines, many confiscations of postcards inartistically depicting the sexual act, and books of humorless and smutty jokes. But these were not the criteria of success. The censorial mind to be content must, as Fitzgerald pointed out, remove from circulation what it does not understand and what therefore angers it. From the vice society's point of view the decade had not been a triumph.

BOSTON, CENSORS' DELIGHT

THE Boston Watch and Ward Society altogether had a better time of it, having achieved the unique feat of coercing the booksellers into the field of censorship. So intimidated were the latter that if the society had disbanded Boston censorship would have taken care of itself. These timorous merchants once censored thirty or forty books at no suggestion from anyone, books the society allowed and the squeamish citizens of Boston did not object to.

There was considerable justification for their attitude. The Massachusetts state law provided that not the publisher or the author is responsible for the obscenity of a book, but the seller. In addition they were jittered by Watch and Ward, more powerful booksellers, Catholic sentiment, by fear of losing customers, by the shady reputation arrest would bring even if followed by acquittal.

The society had once given them cause for trembling. Early in the nineteen-hundreds when the obscenity law was passed, Watch and Ward was as energetic a crackdowner as Comstock's organization in its salad days. For the first ten years after the law went into effect, nearly every bookseller in Boston was arrested and given a minimum fine of one hundred dollars on the complaint of the society (one conviction was made on the charge of selling Rabelais).

An aversion to jailing and fines finally led the merchants

to a truce with their oppressors. Richard F. Fuller of the Old Corner Book Store suggested that a combination committee be formed, consisting of three sellers and three society members, to pass judgment on books of doubtful nature. This was done and he was made chairman. Under the new system the society asked for no arrests until the committee had checked the book in question and, if they turned it down, had sent notice to the trade to this effect and given the merchants three days to act on the hint. The notices were suavely worded with no suggestion of threat, but sellers lost no time clearing out from their shops copies of the objectionable book. The system had suddenly become ironclad, and only a few hardy merchants bucked it to risk jail sentences. The police were whipped into line and agreed to take no action against books without consultation with the committee; this was after they had been so bold as to arrest two women for selling a book that had been passed by the committee. The district attorney was likewise persuaded to work with the committee.

The thing that made the ship of suppression absolutely watertight is not to the credit of American journalism. The two leading papers of Boston agreed to refuse advertisements of books banned by the committee, and their reviewers did not give notices to these books. Thus suppression in Boston was a far sterner thing than suppression in New York, where reviews and notices of actions against a book gave a person a fair chance to procure it if he desired.

The Sumner of Boston was the Reverend J. Frank Chase, who, aside from being one of the founders of 'preventive criticism' (his name for the work of the censorship committee), was author of a handbook for moral crusaders, *The 'Dope' Evil*. The Reverend Mr. Chase abandoned Methodist pulpits in 1907 to take the secretaryship of Watch and Ward, where his first move was to suppress Elinor Glyn's *Three Weeks*. Concerning this he said in 1925 to an interviewer: 'I know you wouldn't make a fool of me, mister, but I have been re-reading *Three Weeks* recently. Do you know I couldn't get a conviction against that book nowadays? I wouldn't dare take it into court!'

Those he dared take to court and procured convictions for: Robert Keable's *Simon Called Peter* and *Numerous Treasure*, *A Young Girl's Diary* (the introduction by Freud may have caused to be banned a book called by *The Nation* as innocent as *Little Women*), *The Satyricon*, *The Decameron* of Boccaccio, Ben Hecht's *Gargoyles*, W. F. Robie's *The Art of Love*, Harland William Long's *Sane Sex Life*, Anderson's *Many Marriages*, Paul Jordon Smith's *Cables of Cobweb*, Floyd Dell's *Janet March*, Warner Fabian's *Flaming Youth* and *Sailors' Wives*, John Dos Passos' *Streets of Night*, Aldous Huxley's *Antic Hay*, Lawrence Rising's *Proud Flesh*, Claude Farrère's *Thomas the Lambkin*, Herbert S. Gorman's *Gold by Gold*, Maxwell Bodenheim's *Replenishing Jessica*, Elliot Paul's *Impromptu*, and *The Price of Things*, *Copulation in the Mammalian Order*, *Sex Happiness*, *Sex Feeling and Living*.

A curious list, but certainly a short one for twenty years of dictatorial censorship. It must be said that after sewing up Boston in a censorship as effective as any ever known, the Reverend Mr. Chase did not take overly much advantage of the situation — for a censor. And further it must be said that at his demise in 1926 his carefully erected system of 'preventive criticism' folded dramatically and its death brought chaos the Reverend never would have permitted. A housewife started it when she surprised her young son reading *The Plastic Age*, and, horrified, told her priest. He went to the authorities with the complaint, and a book which had been published two years before, had reached at least eighty thousand circulation, was suddenly declared obscene.

For some obscure reason this complaint touched off swarms of others, and the sellers-society committee found itself in the unprecedented position of being ignored as a channel of complaint. Boston's complainers, of whom there suddenly seemed to be myriads, took their grievances directly to the police, and Michael Crowley, Superintendent, found himself and his staff deluged in reading matter. The Reverend Mr. Stirling, a retired Episcopal minister of seventy-five, installed himself as chief complainant. He had almost unvarying success in getting convictions except in the case of Rosamond Lehmann's *Dusty Answer*. The Reverend indignantly bore *Dusty Answer* to Charles S. Bodwell, the Watch and Warder who was attempting to keep some semblance of order until the installation of a new secretary.

Bodwell read the book and reported he could find nothing objectionable in it. The churchman said, 'If you can't see it you'd better go to your doctor and get him to tell you.' To which he received the annoyed reply, 'If I have to go to my doctor to find out what's wrong with a book, I guess it won't hurt the general public.' Feeling the police might be more worldly, the Reverend Mr. Stirling took *Dusty Answer* to headquarters, where the copy was dog-eared, rumpled, and torn nearly apart as cops searched its pages for immorality. Miss Lehmann writes subtly, so *Dusty Answer* was not banned in Boston.

The epidemic of purity reached such proportions that book merchants, intimidated anew, sent a small batch of books to the district attorney to ascertain if it was safe to sell them. They were reported to be contrary to the laws of Massachusetts. A few weeks of this indiscriminate pouncing by self-appointed silencers, agitated old ladies, and worried sellers was sufficient to bar as many books as had been suppressed by the Watch and Ward-merchant combine in its entire career. The lot included *The Hard-boiled Virgin* by Frances Newman, *The Marriage Bed* by Ernest Pascal, *The Ancient Hunger* by Edwin Granberry, *Antennae* by Hulbert Footner.

A reporter in search of a story submitted Sinclair Lewis's *Elmer Gantry* to the district attorney; it was barred. The merchants misguidedly attempted a flippancy which only added to the *débâcle*. They sent to the district attorney fifty-seven books. These were just as naughty as those already censored; what was he going to do about it? The harassed official issued a vitriolic statement to the effect that he was tired of using his staff as a censor bureau. They could display the books if they wished, but he was going to ask for jail sentences hereafter. The merchants, feeling their humor had been a mistake, withdrew half the batch. When booksellers ban their own books stranger selections are made than ever the Reverend Mr. Chase and John Sumner could dream of. They picked *Doomsday* by Warwick Deeping, whom one would expect to be a suppressor's favorite author, Jim Tully's *Circus Parade*, Bertrand Russell's *What I Believe*, Lion Feuchtwanger's *Power*, Julia Peterkin's *Black April*, and many more.

While books were being stricken from the lists with such alarming inclusiveness — so that Mencken was provoked to remark, 'It is possible for anyone to have a book suppressed in Boston merely by advancing the idea. I wager I could suppress four books in as many minutes if I should go to Boston and make the effort' — while this deplorable state of affairs existed, the 'art' magazines that were being chased out of many less Puritan cities remained unmolested on Boston news-stands. From 1923 to 1928 the complainers who were bending their energies on legitimate literature never thought to instigate action against them. Pornography vendors thrived in Boston. Mencken, incidentally, was the only opponent of the sellers-society committee who made any appreciable headway against it. He published in *The Mercury* an excellent sketch by Herbert Asbury of a small-town prostitute who every Sunday went penitently to church, where she was refused salvation, so that she bitterly returned to the cemetery where she conducted her business.

The Watch and Ward considered 'Hatrack' too rough and irreligious for perusal by Bostonians, and clamped down on a newsdealer who was handling the magazine. Gleefully Editor Mencken hurried to Boston and had the sport of selling a copy of his *Mercury* to the Reverend Mr. Chase, who promptly had him arrested. Mencken was brought up before a judge who had the intelligence to acquit him on the grounds that a person paying fifty cents for a magazine would not be flooded with lascivious thoughts on reading 'Hatrack.' This test case would have been more effective if a Cambridge judge a week later had not fined a dealer for selling *The Mercury*.

Other suppression-fighters were even less successful. Boni and Liveright went to Boston to get Dreiser's *An American Tragedy* released, but received a one-hundred-dollar fine for their pains. Upton Sinclair, who referred to himself as 'the prize prude of the radical movement, a man who can say he has never told a smutty story,' was hurt and indignant over the suppression of his *Oil*, and put on a small circus in his attempts to get himself arrested, calling meetings to read Act 3, Scene 2, of *Hamlet*, and Genesis, 19, 30–38, to prove Shakespeare and the Bible were much naughtier than he. Publishers, editors, and authors soon gave up in the face of the proved efficacy of Boston's suppressive system; an acceptance of the *status quo* seemed more sensible and less trouble than successful attempts to get arrested and fined.

The wild and unrestrained censorship occurring after the death of the Reverend Mr. Chase was stopped in time to retain a few current books on display. Soon a new secretary for the Watch and Ward was appointed; and after a deal of wangling he persuaded the police to refer complaints to the society as before, and eventually order was restored. The ferocious suppression forced on the civil authorities by individuals demonstrated that for the peculiar conditions existing in Boston the best panacea was control by the Watch and Ward. Boston was in need of a vice society if it was going to have anything to read but the daily papers and pornography.

SUPPRESSION BY THE CHURCH

THE history of literary censorship is entangled with the doings of the Church. It early became evident to the Popes that it would be expedient to keep down heretical reading-matter, which was not an impossible task before the Reformation arrived and with it the invention of the printing press. Blacklists of heretical literature were periodically issued from Rome for the protection of the faithful, and this custom continued until 1930, with the list of Pius the Eleventh, which contained such a huge number of books that it is unlikely if another such list can be compiled. The Catholic Church has not been alone in religious censorship — four years after Queen Mary of England suppressed the work of all Protestant writers, Elizabeth adopted the same measures against Catholic authors — but it has been pre-eminent in this field until the rise of Christian Science.

By the 'twenties Christian Scientists had perfected a machine of suppression that worked with far greater efficiency, diligence, and single-mindedness than the vice societies. Its avowed intention was 'to correct in a Christian manner impositions on the public in regard to Christian Science, injustices done Mrs. Eddy or members of this church by the daily press, by periodicals, or circulated literature of any sort.' It carried out these aims through a committee on publications in each state (two for California). The committee was an individual who looked to a central authority in Boston, and who in turn supervised individuals handling the same work in cities and towns. The work of the committees on publication is best understood by a perusal of extracts from their yearly reports.

Report of the New York Committee on Publications for 1927:

> The Grolier Society, which publishes *The Book of Knowledge*, has accepted a revision of the biography of Mrs. Eddy they have been using.... Funk and Wagnalls, publishers of the *Practical Standard Dictionary* are using Christian Science definitions of words through an arrangement that they have made with the Christian Science Board of Directors. The *Encyclopaedia Britannica* has accepted and published two timely articles, one on Christian Science, and one on Mrs. Eddy. A third one has been submitted and will appear in later printings. This is the result of many years of work with the publishers.

Report of the Illinois Committee on Publications for 1924:

> At the request of this office several book publishers have revised incorrect copy, and one publisher destroyed plates containing disparaging reference to Christian Science. An unauthorized work on Christian Science was removed from circulation at the Chicago Public Library, and an obnoxious textbook in hygiene containing derogatory reference to Christian Science has been withdrawn from use in a university. It is also noteworthy that a plan purporting to accomplish the removal of objectionable books from all public libraries is now receiving the attention of committees on publication.

Report of the New York Committee on Publications for 1925:

> It is seldom that the better papers quibble over printing a correction. To be sure, it is still necessary at times to

emphasize the moral obligation and discreetly to point out the possible legal liability on the part of publishers in connection with the printing of statements misrepresenting the teachings and practice of Christian Science.

Although the Christian Scientists were few in number, a little over two hundred thousand, a large percentage of the membership was wealthy. When a Christian Scientist called upon a managing editor he was likely enough one of the paper's biggest advertisers, and his requests were granted with alacrity. But it was Christian Science zeal and strict adherence to the Church Manual rather than money that accomplished the suppressions desired by the church. Article 8, Section 12 of the Church Manual states, 'A member of this church shall not patronize a publishing house or bookstore that has for sale obnoxious books.' The extent to which Christian Scientists were willing to go to follow this injunction was demonstrated by the case of *Mrs. Eddy: The Biography of a Virginal Mind*, a well-documented and excellently written book by Edwin Franden Dakin.

A BOYCOTT FAILS

CHARLES SCRIBNER'S SONS in the April of 1929 announced this book for early fall publication. The sales force was given confidential memoranda of its selling points. Sometime later Orwell Bradley Towne, Christian

Science publication committee for New York, called upon Scribner's with the request that this book not be printed, saying the sales memoranda showed it to be false and misrepresentative. How Towne acquired a sales memorandum is not known. Scribner's courteously refused his request, and continued preparations for publication. Other calls and letters from Christian Scientists were received by Scribner's, but August 16, 1929, Dakin's book was issued.

Immediately a rain of protest descended upon the publishers and booksellers who stocked the book. The publication committees ostensibly had nothing to do with this, but the official protest centered in Kansas City and St. Louis, and it is unreasonable to suppose that Christian Scientists in those cities were more indignant over the book than other Christian Scientists. Pouring into Scribner's office with uncomfortable regularity and frequency were letters of this sort:

> After reading the review of a book that you have just published called *Mrs. Eddy: The Biography of a Virginal Mind* by E. F. Dakin, I wish to inform you that I, for one, will never patronize your shop again and if there is any way that I can keep others from buying books at your store I will endeavor to do so.

That the program against booksellers met with success in some sections of the country is shown by a letter from the publications committee of Georgia printed in the Macon *Telegraph*:

> We found that the booksellers are as a whole reasonable and fair-minded men. They are not interested in assisting the publishers to distribute a malicious, untruthful book, objectionable (because of its misrepresentations) to many of their fellow-citizens.

These reasonable and fair-minded men were writing desperate letters to Scribner's. Said one: 'A good friend of mine who is a prominent Scientist advises me not to stock the book, stating that it is extremely detrimental to Christian Science, and that if we offered the book for sale our store would be shunned by all local Scientists.' Another letter remarked hopelessly, 'The Christian Scientists are giving us no rest'; and still another averred, 'I have been forced by the Christian Scientists here to put copies I have of *Mrs. Eddy* under the table and to refrain from buying any more.'

In Pittsburgh the Carnegie Library kept Dakin's book from the shelves open to visitors and did not place the title on the monthly list of new books, though in the circulation department *Mrs. Eddy* was carried and was much in demand. Wherever Christian Scientists had influence libraries were doing the same, though in some cases *Mrs. Eddy* was not admitted to the circulating libraries. One of the country's largest and most influential newspapers did not print a review until the book had become such an issue that the omission became conspicuous. Many booksellers were bedeviled into acquiescence, and not only did not carry *Mrs. Eddy* but gave up handling Scribner's books altogether.

Scribner's business was considerably battered, but it did not wage its laudable war alone. *Editor and Publisher* expressed its disapproval of Christian Science suppressive activities. Critics who had hailed *Mrs. Eddy* as one of the best biographies of the year were not content to see suppression crack down upon it — or any book — and they shifted their attention from the works of Watch and

Ward and the New York Society for the Suppression of Vice and directed baleful blasts at church censorship. *The Nation* and *The New Republic* released raucous and telling howls throughout the entire affair, and the former got large glee from the refusal of the *Christian Science Monitor* to print an advertisement of *The Nation's* series of articles, 'The Christian Science Censor.' Some booksellers nobly decided to sell *Mrs. Eddy* even if they were forced out of business. This rallying 'round had the desired effect, and to show they had not been beaten Scribner's about eight months after publication of *Mrs. Eddy* brought out an edition containing new material.

Although Scribner's certainly did not deal a death-blow to Christian Science censorship of books, it did, by sticking steadfastly to its intention to fight the thing through and not relinquish its publishing rights for the pleasure of two tenths of one per cent of the population of the United States, do a good deal to weaken this machine of suppression. Christian Scientists have not pointed the finger of boycott at the publishers of a book of any literary merit since the Scribner's affair.

DEATHBED SCENE

THE obscenity experts, however, suffered a much more shattering tumble at the end of the decade.

In New York, Sumner found the Comstock Act becoming more impotent in regard to higher-bracket books as each of the vice society's actions came to naught. Judges, he saw with consternation, were handing down increasingly liberal opinions as they threw his cases out of court. In 1920 comstockery had taken a bad wallop when the Appellate Division reversed a conviction on the publishing house of Harper's for the publication of *Madeleine, an Autobiography*, saying, 'No one can read this book and truthfully say that it contains a single word or picture which tends to excite lustful or lecherous desire.' Thus the secretary of New York's vice society found that nothing was obscene which did not tend to excite lustful desire — a misinterpretation of the statute, according to Sumner.

That was nothing to the blow, near the end of the 'twenties, contained in another reversal of decision: 'No work may be judged from a selection of such paragraphs alone. Printed by themselves they might, as a matter of law, come within the prohibition of the statute. So might a similar selection from Aristophanes, or Chaucer, or Boccaccio, or even from the Bible. The book, however, must be considered broadly as a whole.' For years Sumner and the other take-actioners had simply dog-eared pages containing sinful passages, read these in court, or submitted them to judge or jury. That had been sufficient until this revolutionary opinion fell from judicial tongue, to the extreme pleasure of suppression's opponents, who felt that this advance was in a fair way to shatter literary censorship. It is difficult to place a book of merit upon the stand and find it obscene in entirety.

The decision on *Mademoiselle de Maupin* made further inroads on New York's statute on obscenity. It established that perversion does not necessarily connote obscenity. Surely John Sumner had reason to grieve at what the 'thirties might bring.

In Boston censorship's disintegration was more spectacular. It revolved around a single case. A clerk of the Dunster House Bookshop was arrested for selling an outlaw book, though he had procured it second-hand at some reluctance at the urging of a disguised Watch and Warder. James A. Delacey, sales manager, also was arrested and convicted.

The Boston intellectuals, who had been the quietest and most acquiescent intellectuals of the country, suddenly grew irate, and Harvard students, who had been the most lamblike and well-behaved of students, fulminated about stupidity and injustice. All the Boston papers but the *Post* evacuated the Watch and Ward camp, and the *Herald* became so bold as to point out editorially that a number of the Watch and Ward agents had criminal records. When Delacey was found guilty under Massachusetts law, the judge carefully explained that 'the Court entertains no cordiality for the society.' Bishop William Lawrence of the Episcopal Church resigned the vice-presidency of the society and Professor Julian Coolidge and Doctor David Scannell resigned from the board of directors.

With its power melting like June hailstones, the Watch and Ward went into long conferences, holding closed meetings which netted reporters nothing. Clearly something had to be done, but the best the society could evolve was a defense prepared for circulation which, after citing Watch and Ward's good works, pleaded, 'It is entitled to be treated with some respect.'

Finally, the Massachusetts obscenity law was changed so that 'a book...containing obscene, indecent, or impure language' could not be banned, but only 'a book... which is obscene, indecent, or impure.' The anti-censors had attempted to get the phrase 'considered as a whole' before the word 'obscene,' but were quite joyous over the compromise, which was actually a sizable triumph for them.

The 'thirties brought release of several books on sex education such as Doctor Marie Stopes's *Married Love*; crudities of expression now are allowed in fiction; classics which speak glowingly of the pleasures of infidelity are no longer expurgated; sex education tracts may go through the mails, and homosexuality does not cause a flitter of censorial eyelashes. *Ulysses* came out of its fifteen-year retirement, brought on when Sumner's society prosecuted *The Little Review* for printing it serially. Its re-emergence seemed to mark the end of an era.

IV. LIGHTER MOMENTS

IV. LIGHTER MOMENTS

Oncoming antiquaries, I suspect, will not ever give us sophisticated writers of the 'twenties our due credit for the pains with which we learned to converse in drawing-rooms about brothels and privies and homosexuality and syphilis and all other affairs which in our first youth were taboo.

BRANCH CABELL: *These Restless Heads*

THE expatriates did not corner all the gaiety. Members of the new literary generation who were too broke or disinclined to live anywhere other than the America they reviled, when they finished the day's work of censor-sniping and nose-thumbing at the academicians had as glad a time as the frequenters of Montmartre.

If you can remember pre-depression days you remember how whirling life was, how lively and new-seeming. Idols were shot down daily, values turned somersaults, and when the greeting 'What's new?' became popular it had some point in a world of huge headlines. The blasé attitude was popular, but secretly no one was bored — it would have been like being bored in the midst of battle. Whoever you were, the world was your oyster. Opportunity knocked twenty-four hours a day, and it was as hard to be a failure as it is now to get a job. Socially and economically the decade was a long feverish celebration, with no thought for the severe hangover the 'thirties must bring.

The 'womanly' woman became as obsolete as the buggy. The nurse must tend the children, the cook must order the meals — life must be spectacular, not frittered away in little household dullnesses. Lips must be brightened, cocktails shaken, a bawdy story told, a hot dance danced. Skirts flourished around and above knees, middle-aged faces were 'lifted' into forgotten loveliness, backs of evening dresses dropped vertebra by vertebra, under-things became fewer and more seductive, and naïveté was a sin.

THE DECLINE OF MANNERS

THE period which made a best-seller out of Emily Post's *Etiquette* paradoxically brought manners into disrepute. It was 'smarter' to be pert than gracious, and 'crashing the gate' was a legitimate social procedure. A party was no good if it was not rowdy; a summer's night in Indianapolis marked the birth of the games of Ring Around the Gin Bottle and Drop the Panties; every frat house acquired tales of spectacular and mixed gatherings in such unexpected places as shower-bath rooms, and Dorothy Parker, the most famous and quoted of the decade's wise-crackers, said of Yale that if all the girls at the prom were laid end to end nobody would be at all surprised.

And people drank. They drank hard and quickly as though each drink might be the last. In the early days of prohibition this was probable, but no one you knew was smitten by poisoned whiskey, and the knowledge that it did, on occasion, blind or kill gave a devilish, reckless air to drinking. The fact that speakeasies were frequented by the gangster-proprietor's gunmen but added to an evening's zest. People made agonized faces over beverages called Scotch, rye, and corn, but nobody really minded the horror of the taste; good liquors seemed effete, and 'prohibition babies' refused wine in favor of cheap gin from the little place down the block.

EXTREMES OF EXTRAVAGANCE

I N THIS gaudy life the *literati* played an untraditional part. They abandoned scholastic seclusion to behave as other men, to an intensified degree. When divorce became fashionable writers changed wives and husbands with extraordinary rapidity. They drank more than other citizens, showing the same eagerness to get happily and quickly plastered as members of the newspaper profession, to which most of them had once belonged. When free love rose to an honorable estate they were among the first to savor its advantages and disillusions. As speech grew franker, they conversed more freely and knowingly than other persons on hitherto unmentionable subjects, employing hitherto unmentionable words. They knew better and dirtier stories, their parties were more hilarious

— in all things they were more extravagant in an extravagant era.

Everything was done to extremes. One publisher's parties in his New York house, with an orchestra and large bar on each of the several floors, were models for the celebrations of other publishers and authors who could afford such lavishness. When notice came that Sinclair Lewis had won the Nobel Prize his friends gathered for congratulations and did not cease festivities for several days, though Lewis, dazed by the award, remained absolutely sober through it all. At an Authors' League dinner Ellis Parker Butler (who once received eighteen toothbrushes from the Prophylactic Brush Company in gratitude for his burlesque Greek novel concerning the characters Halitosis and Prophylactic) indulged in a mock prize-fight refereed by Dorothy Gish resplendent in a pair of red pants, and children's games were alcoholically enjoyed by the assembled writers, who playfully tossed about balloons in the interims. The custom of attending one's own parties was outlawed in literary circles when Sinclair Lewis did not show up at Jean and Herbert Gorman's studio, where he was presumably entertaining, and a woman literary agent telephoned her dinner guests, gathered to meet a novelist, that she had decided not to come.

The revolution in manners was evident in working life as well as in social. Hergesheimer was a sought-after lecturer before women's clubs until he opined to them that a marcel is the chief difference between women and other animals, and other such heresies. He created a sensation at Yale when he arrived on the speaker's platform to find women in the audience and could think of nothing else to talk about but his prepared topic, 'The Feminine Nuisance in Literature.' Criticism crossed the bounds of frankness and became on occasion exceedingly rude. Reviewers made libelous deductions as to the personal lives of authors, accusing them of bad taste and caddishness. A famous woman author in reviewing another woman author's book said: 'I have often wondered how Miss —— would have treated sex if, instead of being a woman of impeccable virtue, she had chosen to be a *dame galante*.'

Log-rolling was prevalent, and few writers carried ethics to the point of refusing a hand up to someone whose friendship could be of any value. Throat-cutting was equally popular. A critic for a New York paper wrote an unfavorable review of a book and contributed unsigned copies gratis to two other papers because he had once met the author and thought him 'too fresh.' When Floyd Dell in a piece in *The Bookman* disparagingly discussed a poet without naming him, Cale Young Rice immediately sprang into print with 'The animosity of Mr. Dell is wholly personal. When a young man he sent me some of his verses for criticism and my kindly efforts to help him were inadequate to the demands of his vanity. From that time to the present he has lost no opportunity to vent his resentment.' After Dell wrote Rice to say he had not referred to him, all was forgiven — but the incident was typical of the decade's touchiness.

RECREATION PERIOD

THE Algonquin Hotel was to the New York literary people what Schlogl's restaurant was to Chicago writers. Schlogl's became famous when authors and critics began dropping in on Saturday afternoons, grouping themselves around a big round table to indulge in talk and food. The Algonquin was literary twenty-four hours a day, its register jammed with visiting celebrities and its dining-room filled at the lunch hour with most of the writers in New York. The lobby was crowded with spectators who came to view literary notables in much the same way a Parisian bookstore proprietor hoped they would when he opened an adjoining grill-room and invited writers to attend. Most of these celebrity-gazers were feminine, of the lion-hunting breed, of whom Ernest Boyd has written that their genius lies in an infinite capacity for taking pains to keep in the swim. These purposeful ladies also dined frequently at the Brevoort, on the fringe of Greenwich Village, which lured writers with superb food as well as with the presence of other writers.

The era marked the rise of the literary tea, that pleasant custom comprised of a great many cocktails and a little business. To a really ambitious tea would be invited most of the New York critics, prominent and not-so-prominent authors, literary agents, publishers, and a sprinkling of people with no connection with the writing business but who managed through their good looks (in the case of women), wit, or persistence to be in demand.

Most literary teas ostensibly were given for the purpose of honoring distinguished visiting writers, but in the course of the festivities, before the younger and more raucous element got themselves cock-eyed, quite a tidy bit of business and good-willing was accomplished. In the crowd of regular tea-goers, assiduously attending nearly every literary gathering in Manhattan, figured John and Margaret Farrar, Carl and Irita Van Doren, Ernest Boyd, Isabel Paterson, W. E. and Helen Woodward, Henry Hazlitt, Harry Hansen, Lewis Gallantière, Harry Salpeter, William Rose Benét, Elinor Wylie, and Henry Seidel Canby.

Festivities made the accomplishment of work difficult. Heywood Broun finally inaugurated the custom of taking a month's vacation a year; he emerged from two with two finished novels. Much of the output was planned in pleasantly social surroundings, as in the case of *Civilization in the United States*, which the eminent contributors (among them Mencken and Nathan) met to discuss in the rickety Greenwich Village house of Harold Stearns, editor of the symposium. Gathered in a small, tumbled room, they talked of everything but their project and finally adjourned the meetings to some nearby dance place. Dorothy Parker, whose verse utters cynicism as prettily and sharply as it has ever been uttered, had such an aversion to work that it is alleged she put the sign 'Gentlemen' over the door of her one-room office, thereby ensuring an unusual number of visitors. Miss Parker's *Enough*

Rope and *Sunset Gun*, two verse collections, made her revered by young sophisticates, most of whom overlooked the exquisitely bitter poems in favor of those flippancies such as the one which ends

> But I, despite expert advice,
> Keep doing things I think are nice,
> And though to good I never come —
> Inseparable my nose and thumb!

(A heavy-handed paraphrase was made by Alfred Stieglitz, the genius photographer and discoverer of literary talents, in his 'Spiritual America,' a close-up view of the stern side of a horse.)

A more strenuous means of recreation than talking and drinking was found in walking trips. Thornton Wilder hiked off with Gene Tunney, the heavy-weight champion, with such a publicized liking for Shakespeare that he was pictured in *The New Yorker* reading a book upside down; as did Sinclair Lewis and W. E. Woodward. They were wise enough to keep on foreign shores and so avoid the fate of Burton Rascoe and a friend, who were much twitted on their walking trip to end walking trips. They trudged along for several days, taxiing to a boat in New York, disembarking at a port city to taxi to a train, and finally dropping off the train at the city of their destination into a third taxi, which deposited the weary walkers at a friend's home.

The book fair was a phenomenon inaugurated in the 'twenties. Its purpose was to bring the world of books and authors into closer social touch with the general public. This ingenious idea was adopted by Marcella Burns, head of the book department of Marshall Field and Company, who had observed its popularity in German cities and persuaded her employers to put on one in Chicago. It was an immediate success, with a hundred thousand persons flocking to view the manuscripts of Daisy Ashford, Tennyson, Kipling, and Mark Twain, the thirty-five-hundred-dollar jewel-encrusted edition of Keats, and the many publishers, writers, and poets, the biggest hit of whom was Eddie Guest, who autographed until his arm was lame.

Observing Marshall Field's triumph, other book and department stores quickly put on their own fairs, to which the public responded with equal enthusiasm. Not only people interested in books and writers came, but rafts of others eager to meet, handshake, and chat with celebrities who were amiably giving autographs to all comers. (It was a hardly incidental part of the fairs that the public, thrilled by the literary atmosphere, bought considerable numbers of books.) Clubwomen descended on fairs in droves, each eager to snare some prominent writer out of the fair into her club and onto the lecture platform, or better still, into her home where she could throw a select dinner and impress her fellow bathers in the social swim.

Literary lionization is an old business, but it was uncommonly popular in the 'twenties, thriving on so fierce a competition that many writers followed Sherwood Anderson's lead in refusing to be entertained by club hostesses.

Among the most sought-after speakers was distinguished-looking John Erskine, who enthralled the ladies with a careful mixture of seriousness and suave naughtiness. Aristocratic Bertrand Russell made quite a business of lecturing, although he did have a disheartening experience at one Middle-Western university. His talk was called off because the gymnasium, the only auditorium, had to be utilized for a basket-ball game. Floyd Dell's first-hand knowledge of Greenwich Village made him a popular speaker, and F. Scott Fitzgerald drew crowds of flappers (a term which he claimed Mencken invented) whenever he could be persuaded to the lecture platform.

Anderson, a superb *raconteur* in private life, was shy when talking in public. To get over those first embarrassed moments he invented a stock opening which ran, 'I am not really an author — I am a business man.' This formula was successful until his acceptance speech at the *Dial* prize dinner. One irritated *Dial* editor was driven to mutter to a neighbor, 'We didn't award the *Dial* prize to a *business man*.'

'Culture' became suddenly popular in the 'twenties. A laundry company's delivery trucks displayed a picture of a happy if somewhat moronic-looking woman saying, 'I send my clothes to the Ideal Laundry. It leaves more time for culture.' Haldeman-Julius, 'the Henry Ford of publishing,' was cashing in gloriously in his ten-cent 'Blue Books,' a library containing everything from philosophy to directions for becoming an expert carpenter. This appetite for information created a widespread demand for lecturers, chiefly on the part of women's clubs, which needed them as an excuse for weekly or monthly gatherings. (There were some clubs like the one in Central City, Kentucky, which relied on members for addresses; *The Mercury* quoted a report that 'one of the most cultural programmes ever given by the Woman's Club was enjoyed by its members at the home of Mrs. Clarence Martin, on Main Street. Mrs. Eaves gave, in her own fluent way, a very instructive talk on "How to Use the Victrola.")

Since literature was regarded as about the most cultural thing going, an entertainment committee which lassoed a writer was considered more successful than one which produced a painter or musician. It did not matter very much what the writer selected for a subject or how he treated the subject as long as he was charmingly deferential to the intelligence of the audience and passably good to look upon. For most of the ladies, it must be admitted, had no more taste for literature than the man on shipboard who pressed his lips to a copy of one of Harold Bell Wright's novels and assured William McFee it was the greatest book in the world. Although there is well-documented evidence that one culture club spent twenty-three years studying Shakespeare and another devoted twenty-three to Dickens, most of them considered a writer — whether Tolstoi or Faith Baldwin — disposed of in an hour.

The significance of the culture clubs paled when the depression arrived; lectures on such subjects as the fifteenth-century Polish poets seemed less important when money was so short and there was so much to be done at home. Likewise the conviviality of the literary brethren faded as the economic world wabbled ominously. For financial and spiritual reasons it was necessary to do quickly a great deal of work and do it well, a procedure not compatible with constant attendance at the Algonquin dining-room and every literary tea and writers' binge held in New York. A new and quite unaccustomed seriousness descended on the now-graying younger generation of 1920, so that auctorial social life, although still far brighter and less predictable than that of other persons, fell into its proper category from the status of a full-time job.

V. THRILLING! MAGNIFICENT! ASTOUNDING!

V. THRILLING! MAGNIFICENT!
ASTOUNDING!

I should here like to expose certain literary fragments, torn
jaggedly from the hard contexts, fragments which, being
felt out with the hammer of our intellects, return the
consistency of rock crystal, fragments which, being thrown
upon the hearth of our sympathetic understanding, betray
the immense, the salt-veiled, the profoundly meditated
chromatization of enkindled driftwood.

Schofield Thayer, discussing Marianne Moore in *The
Dial* of February, 1925.

IF THERE is any truth in Anatole France's celebrated
remark that criticism is the adventure of the soul
among masterpieces, the critics of the new generation
had a better life than any of their predecessors. At least
one of them proclaimed practically every novel that
appeared 'a masterpiece.'

Each decade is tagged with an adjective. The 'twenties
was the age of superlatives. Advertisers found that even
the word 'best' lost its meaning after a while, and we got
such synthetic superlatives as 'throat-ease,' 'sealed-in
goodness,' 'beauty-rest,' and 'not a cough in a carload.'
From Hollywood came 'gigantic masterpiece' and 'super-
thriller.' Vaudeville managers billed acts as 'added attractions' and 'special extra added attractions.' Even
gasoline filling stations became 'super-service stations.'
In conversation things were 'swell' or 'lousy,' with only
rarely an intermediate rating.

In literary criticism the same easy and violent opinions prevailed. More persons were professing the art in the 'twenties than at any time before. Book sections and book columns became a standard feature of the majority of newspapers with more than seventy-five thousand circulation. American editors had at last discovered the truth in the late Lord Northcliffe's remark that there are as many good news stories in books as in police court. Companionate marriage, the debunking of historical figures, and other themes of books of the 'twenties offered the novelty city editors are eternally looking for, and writers made quite as much news as if they had gone around biting dogs. Richard Halliburton swam the Hellespont; Fannie Hurst and her husband lived apart and made 'dates' to see each other, claiming this the ideal system of marriage.

Book news thus became more exciting than reports of Congress, if still less exciting than the accounts of divorce trials, and writers became sufficiently well known to have their names spelled correctly in the news columns. As publishers increased their advertising appropriations, book sections and columns acquired an added journalistic virtue. Never did they make as much money as the Sunday automobile and the Friday food pages — sixty per cent advertising and forty per cent publicity — but many of them paid their own way.

These sections were usually edited by critics who entered the field with little of the equipment a professor of the art is traditionally supposed to possess — wide reading, a grounding in the classics, the maturity without which balanced judgment is usually impossible. An enthusiasm for books and the kind of egoism or egotism which can be satisfied only by seeing one's name in print — these were frequently the only qualifications, plus, of course, the ingenuity to get a job. Most of them were excitable children of the age of superlatives, and to their natural inclination for word-sprees was added the fact that they could get their names in advertisements and on dust jackets — and therefore perhaps a better job — if they shouted loudly enough.

And so the reviewers filled their reviews with such words as 'magnificent,' 'stirring,' 'thrilling,' 'saga,' 'epic,' and 'monumental,' with the abandon of a tipsy American collegian spending papa's francs in Montmartre. The search for new pinnacles of praise was to go on until by the end of the decade reviewers were using the newspaper term 'must' to tell their customers that a reading of the book under discussion was obligatory, or were abandoning the English language altogether and simply printing * * * after a title. By 1921 the tendency had gone so far that Heywood Broun issued a formal warning:

> The young critic's gaudiest years [he wrote] come early in life. Middle age and beyond are apt to be tragic. Almost nothing in the experience of mankind is quite so heart-rending as the spectacle of one of these young critics, grown gray, coming face to face in his declining years with a masterpiece. At such times he is apt to be seized with a tremor and stricken dumb. Undoubtedly he is tormented with the memory of all the adjectives which he flung away in his youth. They are gone beyond recall. He fumbles in his purse and finds nothing except small change worn smooth. The best he can do is to fling out a 'highly creditable piece of work' and go on his way.

It was a sensible warning. Nobody paid any attention to it.

Worse, the critics who were entitled to practice the art both by reason of their ability and a genuine demand for their work succumbed at times to the urge for overstatement. The files of newspapers and magazines are filled with such dicta as Louis Bromfield's that *No More Parades* by Ford Madox Ford was 'as great as anything produced in English during the past twenty-five years,' Burton Rascoe's that Viña Delmar's *Bad Girl* was 'one of the miracles of American life,' Percy Hutchison's that *A Modern Comedy* by John Galsworthy was 'one of the great fictions of literature, a truly stupendous and astounding work,' William Lyon Phelps's that Thornton Wilder was 'an artist of the first rank, original and profound, literally the last word,' and Herbert Gorman's that *Dodsworth* by Sinclair Lewis was 'a book that impresses us again with the potentialities of Sinclair Lewis as an American Balzac.'

This comparison of American writers with the European masters was a favorite device of those who were unable or unwilling to dissect the book at hand and struggle to reveal to the reader what it was like. In advertising *Wolf Solent*, a pretentious book by the Englishman John Cowper Powys, the publishers noted that 'scores of reviewers, seeking standards of comparison, have fallen back on Poe, Tolstoi, Wordsworth, Shakespeare and Dickens.'

Save for the degree of extravagance in the use of adjectives and the name of the European master chosen for comparison, most newspaper criticism became stereotyped and wooden. Tragedy was always 'intense,' 'moving,' 'real,' 'stirring,' or 'emotional'; comedy was 'sparkling,' 'bright,' 'merry,' 'mirth-provoking,' or 'gloom-dispelling'; the treatment of sex was 'fearless,' 'frank,' or 'challenging.' The majority of reviews thus offered the novel-reader little information of any value about the books that were being published, and the advertisements of them took on the appearance of circus posters. Any book advertised was likely to be trailed by quotations from reviews announcing it to be a 'masterpiece,' 'a saga,' or an 'epic,' and quotations from panegyrics mailed out by publishers' press agents were printed unedited in chatter columns on the book pages.

This lazy attitude of book editors led to some amusing situations, as when a press agent, copying encomiums of a new book, quoted a reviewer as saying: 'So absorbed was I that I forgot the proximity of the stove, up to which I was huddled. Imagine my surprise when I found I had burned a large hole in my trousers.' The press agent forgot to copy the name of the author of this tribute, but followed it immediately with one from another reviewer. The two appeared in a newspaper as the comment of a woman.

CLOSING IN ON TRADITION

NOT all the criticism was silly, and many of the critics brought to their task learning, wit, diligence, and conscientiousness. The decade of paradoxes which gave us some of the poorest criticism America had seen also gave us some of the best. There was criticism, as Mary Austin pointed out, by 'the foreign or foreignly derived writer acquiring that detailed familiarity with American life which is demanded by creative literature.' There were critics who, in James Branch Cabell's tolerant phrase of dismissal, were reviewing books only because they had not had time to finish books of their own. There were critics who were criticizing 'for the hell of it.' But there were also men and women to whom criticism was itself a worthy career, whose taste and literary skill lent luster to the literature of the decade — Laurence Stallings, Mencken, Paul Rosenfeld, Carl Van Doren, Henry Seidel Canby, John Macy, Broun, Harry Hansen, Ernest Boyd, John Farrar, Stuart Sherman, Burton Rascoe, Francis Hackett, Wilson Follett, Edmund Wilson, Isabel Paterson, Alexander Woollcott, Van Wyck Brooks, and a few others.

The work of these critics was of uneven quality, and they approached their job with widely disparate critical theories. The decade, in fact, saw much criticism of criticism, as it witnessed the birth of advertising of advertising, but there was no unity of opinion as to what criticism was, or why it existed. Rascoe told his readers that 'the value of literary criticism lies in the amount of antagonism or appreciation I can stir in you by an expression of opinion about a book.' To Floyd Dell, a young rebel who by 1922 had incurred the wrath of a still younger generation, 'all criticism was motivated by jealousy and envy.'

Joel Elias Spingarn conceived of the critic as a creative artist, and at times this notion appealed to Mencken.

'No matter how artfully the critic may try to be impersonal and scientific,' Mencken wrote, 'he is bound to give
himself away. I am a critic of books, and through books
of *Homo sapiens*, and through *Homo sapiens* of God.'
But in another mood Mencken conceived of the critic as
a mere human catalytic agent, bringing the reader to the
book and himself remaining completely impersonal.

Of varying critical theories and degrees of seriousness,
the leading critics of the decade had a great deal in common. With the exception of Sherman they rejected the
arid traditionalism allegedly confessed by Brander Matthews, until 1922 editor of the New York *Times* book section, in the remark that an insult to Emerson was an insult to him. Emphatically they rejected the dictum of
Jules Lemaître that 'criticism of our contemporaries is
not criticism, it is only conversation.' The leading critics
of the period had a keen and driving interest in their
contemporaries, and belligerently asserted the right to
assess them. If their preoccupation with books of modern
authorship led them at times to excesses and untenable
pronouncements, this was better than the old half-
ashamed colonial attitude of earlier American critics toward the productions of their contemporaries.

American criticism of the period — that is, criticism in
the higher brackets — had a fresh, pop-eyed, exciting,
unself-conscious attitude that was lacking in the criticism
before the decade dawned, when books were being assayed
by such comparatively dull and unimaginative men as
Doctor Maurice Francis Egan, Austin Hay, Matthews,
Richard Le Gallienne, John Walcott, and P. H. Boynton.
Critics, far from pigeonholing and endeavoring to cor-

relate new ideas with the literature of the past, greeted novelty with shouts of enthusiasm. Whatever seemed interesting and fresh got a hearing. Free alike from the notion that art should inculcate a moral, which Edgar Allan Poe spent his life combatting, and the notion that form was more important than substance, they weighed books according to their worth as critiques of life, as purveyors of entertainment. The robust literature of the period got the kind of criticism it needed for encouragement, if it did not get sufficient restraining advice.

Critics, even the best of them, praised a good deal of trash in terms which would be embarrassing for them to recall now, but they did battle also for all that was vital and worth-while in the output of the younger generation. If revolt was the midwife which produced many of the best writers of the decade, criticism was the nurse which fended for them in the literary world.

'A BAD WRITER HAS NO RIGHTS'

HENRY LOUIS MENCKEN was the most persevering nurse of them all. As an editor, first of *Smart Set* and then of *The American Mercury*, he encouraged every writer of promise who submitted a manuscript. No offering of any worth was sent back with a formal rejection slip; Mencken out of the kindness of his heart and his genuine interest in writing managed to find time to ease

the author's disappointment with at least a brief note.
'What other ideas have you?' was the encouraging question that sent many of them back to their typewriters to
try again. When the writers he discovered or helped to
discover were launched, Mencken as a critic prodded
them to do more and better work, helped to find publishers for them, and demanded attention for them when
their books appeared. If Van Vechten created more fads
than any other literary man of his time, Mencken was to
some degree responsible for more successes.

Kind as well as vastly intelligent, Mencken has nevertheless created a bitter, violent, and scurrilous band of
enemies. Few men in the history of the country, not even
excluding Aaron Burr, have been abused with such persistence and rancor. He has been called 'a maggot, a
ghoul of new-made graves, a buzzard' (Tampa *Times*);
'a jackal '(Jackson, Mississippi, *News*); 'a dog that bites
the hand that feeds it' (Camden, New Jersey, *Courier*);
'a pole-cat' (San Francisco *Chronicle*); and 'a wasp'
(Minneapolis *Journal*). A writer in the Concord, New
Hampshire, *Monitor* remarked that 'if Mencken only ran
about on all fours, slavering his sort of hydrophobia, he
would be shot by the first policeman on duty'; and the
New Haven *Union* said he was 'a treacherous alien sap-
ping at the vitals of America's proudest and most essential
institutions, an indecent buffoon wallowing in obscenity
as he howls with glee.'

Quotations of this kind from magazines, newspapers,
and radio broadcasts would fill volumes. In 1926 four
hundred editorials were printed denouncing him. Mencken
has been excommunicated from the pulpits, boycotted by

libraries, given the 'silent treatment' by college professors; during the World War he was questioned by a secret service agent who seemed to think he was a German spy. Actually he is a pleasant, good-mannered, charitable, and sentimental person, but this depiction of himself as a fiend and intellectual hoodlum does not distress him; to the contrary, it delights him. He revels in the abuse by his inferiors, as many another man would revel in their praise. He keeps copious scrapbooks of the vicious and libelous things said of him, and will go to as much trouble to locate a clipping that vilifies him as to track down new loan words for the next edition of *The American Language*.

This enjoyment is perhaps due less to a boyish yearning to be in the thick of the fight than a feeling that condemnation by his inferiors is an oblique sort of flattery. Mencken has incurred the disapproval of first-rate men, who have expressed that disapproval intelligently and pointedly, but most of his detractors have been of the type he despises: the superstitiously religious, the blindly patriotic, the 'boost-don't-knock' fraternity.

Mencken, who comes of a family that was distinguished in Europe for generations, was born in Baltimore, where he became a reporter at nineteen when his father's death ended his formal schooling. He was instantly successful in journalism, and in two years held an executive position, the Sunday editorship of the *Herald*. Before he was twenty he was selling with some regularity to the magazines, and in 1903, at the age of twenty-three, he published his *Ventures into Verse*, a volume of extremely bad poetry. In later years he tried to destroy all extant copies, but the Library of Congress retained one, and poets whom

Mencken has attacked have often soothed their wounded feelings by reading it and reflecting that Mencken knows nothing about poetry.

Mencken wrote no more verse after the publication of this unfortunate maiden effort, and soon afterward he gave up fiction, a medium in which he was much more successful. Criticism and editing were his fields, and in 1905 he produced a book on George Bernard Shaw which launched him in the former. This book, the completion of which was delayed by arguments between him and Harrison Hale Schaff of John W. Luce and Company over his violent and picturesque expressions, was well received. He followed it with a study of Nietzsche, mastering German in order to go to original sources for his material.

Journalism was beginning to interest him less and less, though he has always retained an active connection with newspapers, and when, through Theodore Dreiser, he became book critic for *Smart Set*, he felt his career was taking the proper turn. For more than fifteen years he wrote literary criticism — monthly articles for *Smart Set* and later for *The American Mercury*, weekly articles for the Baltimore *Evening Sun*, weekly pieces that were syndicated to scores of newspapers, and occasional reviews for *The Nation* and other magazines.

That criticism is the liveliest that America has ever seen. Mencken writes with gusto, with bounce; his style is full of strange but apt figures; he is a master of the sentence that explodes in the end with dazzling and comical effects. His interesting style at once attracted readers to his reviews, and reading them they found an independence of judgment, a capacity to appraise the books before him, that had few precedents in American criticism. They found he was against the dull, the pretentious, the speciously 'arty'; that he was on the side of men and women who could write clearly and move the reader by legitimate means to a dignified emotional response. He was for Mark Twain (this fight was one of his earliest literary victories), and against Thorstein Veblen; he was for Cabell and against O. Henry; he was for James Huneker and against Henry van Dyke. He was for freedom of thought and action, and he fought to cut the chains of traditionalism as hard as he fought to liberate men who were jailed for their opinions.

> As a critic [he wrote after more than a decade of reviewing] I regret nothing. I have made some mistakes, but on the whole I have been on the side of sound artists and against frauds. My judgments, as I look back on them, have been pretty good. The men I was advocating in 1908 are all viewed with respect today; the fakes I then attacked are now forgotten. I have been, at times, very cruel, but I do not regret it. A bad writer has no rights whatever. Any mercy shown him is wasted and mistaken.

Mencken had a vast influence on the literature of the 'twenties — he suggested ideas for numerous books and told authors how to write them — but his influence on criticism was even greater. As the younger fiction-writers rallied around Dreiser, so the younger critics rallied around Mencken. His irreverence, his distrust of cant, his 'joy in what seemed free and bold' were reflected in the criticism of the 'Quality Group' of magazines to only a slightly less degree than in college students' publications and the newspapers. By the time he retired from literary criticism there was a definite Mencken School of criticism.

He retired partly because he was tired of fiction after reading so many thousands of volumes of it (the critical acclaim given a freakish piece of fiction like *Lady into Fox* is largely due to the reviewers' satiety with orthodox performances), and partly because for years he had felt a growing desire to study and discuss such subjects as ethics, government, and sociological problems. Politics has always interested him. Though he is opposed to democracy and regularly denounces office-holders as charlatans and jackasses, he sweats through the boisterous inanity of every national political convention. To Frank Harris he was chiefly important as a critic of politics. Harris wrote:

> To say that Mencken is the best critic in the United States is less than his due; he is one of the best critics in English. In his absorption in criticism alone, and in a certain masculine abruptness and careless piquancy of style, he reminds me of Hazlitt, one of the critics who belong to literature. In regard to creative work, especially to stories and plays, his judgment is often at fault, and always leaves a good deal to be desired; but in dealing with politicians and political issues, how sane he is, how brave, how honest, how surely he finds the fitting word, the blistering epithet!

Since deserting literary criticism, Mencken has produced a work on ethics and a revision of his fascinating and immensely valuable *American Language*.

DECLARATION OF INDEPENDENCE

O F ALL the charges that have been brought against Mencken in his turbulent career, none appears more frequently than the assertion that he is un-American and engaged in undermining our noblest traditions. The Lowell, Massachusetts, *Sun* called him 'a British toady,' the Vancouver, British Columbia, *Sun* a Hungarian, the *Arkansas Democrat* a 'former subject of the German Kaiser,' and the Richmond, Virginia, *Times-Dispatch* concluded that he was 'an outstanding, disgusting example of what constitutes a poor American.' Actually Mencken is as patriotic as a Legionnaire; his rages against intolerance and mediocrity spring from a reformer's impulse to cajole and shame his country into a striving for enlightenment and decency.

Like Poe, Emerson, and Whitman, Mencken has fought for an indigenous American culture, free of imitativeness and dependence, completely and proudly American. Whitman believed 'a great original literature' was 'sure to come,' and Emerson in 1837 proclaimed that 'our day of dependence, our long apprenticeship to the learning of other lands, draws to a close.... Events, actions arise, that must be sung, that will sing themselves.' When Mencken wrote his essay 'The National Letters' in 1920 he saw little hope that America would escape from the 'conformity, timorousness, lack of enterprise and audacity' which he said were the enemies of great literature. As the

decade of revolt began to produce the questioning, unmoral novels of Cabell and Anderson, the earthy studies of
Miss Cather and Miss Suckow, Ring Lardner's and John
V. A. Weaver's explorations of the common American's
speech, and Lewis's vivisections of American business and
religion, Mencken slowly became convinced that the
dreams of Whitman, Poe, Emerson, Oliver Wendell
Holmes, and Van Wyck Brooks were coming true:
America was at last producing a literature as interesting as
any in the world, and a literature that was as American as
apple pie, baseball, and speakeasies.

Other Americans discovered the new independence, and
rejoiced in it. Edna Ferber sounded the call to arms:

> It's time we stopped imitating. It's time we denied this
> libel to the effect we're crude, unformed, and undeveloped.
> Let us write in the American fashion about America. Let's
> paint in the American fashion from American subjects.
> We've got color, and romance, and vivacity, and depth
> all the way from Maine to Manila. . . . Perhaps when we
> begin to respect our art our European fellow artists will
> respect it.

Miss Ferber practiced what she preached to the extent of
living on James Adams's Floating Theater for two months
to get atmosphere for *Show Boat*. The Floating Theater
presented such *opera* as *Why Girls Leave Home*, the crew of
the tug which pulled it around doubled in brass, and the
leading man always appeared before the curtain to thank
the good ladies for the home-made cakes they had sent the
members of the cast. Miss Ferber's novel missed greatness, but it was as native as the dark tragedies of Thomas
Hardy.

Mencken's championship of American literature was seconded by many of the critics of the new generation. It led, in the natural course of controversy, to disparagement of contemporary productions of other countries, and particularly England. Ernest Boyd, reviewing *To Let* by John Galsworthy, *The Thirteen Travelers* by Hugh Walpole, and *Ursula Trent* by W. L. George, ridiculed the theory that a third-rate English novel is necessarily better than a first-rate American one, which he said has always been the basis of criticism in both countries. 'Not one of them,' he said bluntly, 'has anything to say, or perhaps it would be more accurate to suggest that all three want to say the same thing, and each of them says nothing.' He remarked that it was easy to find three current American novels of greater significance and originality.

The English took up the challenge. The London *Mercury* proclaimed that Hergesheimer was the only American novelist of his generation that Englishmen 'were able to admire and to consider seriously.' W. L. George told an interviewer that the important writers produced by America were Frank Norris, Jack London, and Dreiser, which left us only one outstanding living writer; and Henry W. Nevinson added to the carnage by assuring English readers that no critic worthy of the name was practicing in the States.

Into the fray plunged Hugh Walpole when Mencken complained in *The Smart Set* that England ignored the best American writers. Walpole, a handsome and boyish-looking Englishman who probably holds the world's record for fascinating American women at tea-parties, came frequently to this country, and he set himself up as the interpreter of literary America for England. He was one of the early drum-beaters for Cabell, Hergesheimer, and Miss Glasgow, and Mencken's charge annoyed him. In an open letter in *The Bookman* he replied that Cabell, Anderson, Lewis, and Miss Cather were received hospitably in the Mother Country, and in this and a subsequent open letter poked gentle fun at Mencken for his bellicose assertions that American literature was more interesting than English. The controversy was immensely polite, each contestant promising the other his choicest whiskies upon their next meeting, but beneath the surface there were discernible the fierce determination of the child to go his own way, and the sadness of the parent at his going. The Republic, said Mencken, had cut the painter, and never again would look to England for literary guidance.

The critics thus joined the younger novelists in their revolt against Puritanism and Victorianism, and incidentally won at least a surface victory for an autonomous American culture. Perhaps the victory is real. It is certainly true that America no longer looks to England for judgment on its writers. And the notion that an English book is *ipso facto* better than an American one is as dead as the essays of J. G. C. Brainard.

If most of the critics united in reciting the American literary declaration of independence, they were united on little else. In 1922 *Vanity Fair* sent an elaborate questionnaire to critics and tabulated the results in an article which throws revealing light on the men who made our criticism. The replies showed certain critics considered Cézanne, Picasso, and Matisse greater than Raphael, Lenin one of the world's greatest living statesmen, Irving

Berlin a greater composer than Schönberg or Edward MacDowell, William Jennings Bryan a better statesman than Henry Cabot Lodge, and Nietzsche the greatest philosopher of all. They decided the twelve greatest artists and thinkers in history were Shakespeare, Bach, Beethoven, Nietzsche, Wagner, Leonardo, Charlie Chaplin, Flaubert, Aristotle, Plato, Anatole France, and George Washington. There were votes for Krazy Kat, Omar Khayyám, Kant, Rabelais, Babe Ruth, Saint Paul, Wordsworth, and Ed Wynn. Paul Rosenfeld was rated the best equipped in the lot. Heywood Broun, who admired France, Chaplin, Whitman, Ruth, Frueh, Shakespeare, and Shaw, and hated Hearst and the popular evangelist Billy Sunday, was called the most poorly equipped for the critic's robes. 'His answers reveal,' said *Vanity Fair*, 'a meagerness of cultural equipment incredible in a man who with H. L. Mencken is a kind of literary godfather to the rising generation of American *literati*.'

IT SEEMS TO BROUN

HOWEVER poorly he rated on charts, Heywood Broun produced some of the freshest and sanest criticism of the period, and when he, like Mencken, left literature for more 'serious' fields he left a vacancy on the critics' bench which (with no relation to his exceeding corpulence) has never been filled. Broun is very nearly the

ideal journalist of our time. His inclusion of Babe Ruth in
the list of his idols was due to no mere desire to shock: he is
genuinely interested in almost everything that goes on and
in every quirk of personality. Ideas occur to him with incredible frequency, and composition comes easy. Like
Mencken, he has the gift of striking and vivid phrasing,
and a low-comedy sense of humor that glows through his
most serious and indignant passages.

Irreverence is natural to him, as shown by his lead on his
report of a World Series baseball game in which the ageing
Walter Johnson, regarded by sports writers as a has-been,
threw a baseball with the speed which earlier had caused
Ty Cobb to remark that you can't hit 'em if you can't see
'em. Broun began his story: 'Billy Sunday left baseball for
the pulpit, but I had to leave the church for the baseball
diamond to learn the true meaning of the Sermon on the
Mount.' He compared Johnson's achievement with the
resurrection of Christ, and described the throwing of a
third strike by saying, 'The stone had been rolled away.'
Broun was genuinely thrilled by Johnson's amazing come-
back performance, and from it got a lesson on the in-
vincibility of man that made him think, in all innocence, of
the life of Christ.

Broun's passion for baseball — he was graduated from
the sports pages to criticism — is indicative of a certain
boyishness that has remained with him into middle age.
He has always made large sums of money — as a columnist
for the old New York *World* and the New York *Telegram*
and *World-Telegram*, as a lecturer and as a writer of books
— but he frequently finds himself penniless on occasions
that would embarrass more conventional persons. Of

great physical as well as intellectual courage, he is always ready for a fight. He waded in on one occasion to protect a chorus girl who was being jostled in a subway. He had less success another time, when he defended the name of Michael Collins, who was being abused by a soap-box orator; five Irishmen gave him a black eye. He is capable of ridiculing his own efforts, as when he took up painting, and he creates audacious and amusing names for his diversions, such as the well-publicized Thanatopsis and Inside Straight Poker Club.

Broun has written at least four million words for his newspaper columns. No one so prolific could be invariably interesting, but so great is his zest, so catholic his interests, so ingratiating his style that he still ranks with Popeye, Dorothy Dix, and Angelo Patri as one of the most profitable 'properties' in the syndicate business. Despite the demands of daily journalism upon his time and mental energy, he has found time to appear in a revue and to write several books, including *The Boy Grew Older*, *Gandle Follows His Nose*, and, with Margaret Leech, a life of Anthony Comstock in which he submerged his hatred for reformers and wrote a judicial and even kind biography.

Broun was never exclusively a literary critic, but in the early 'twenties he reviewed fairly regularly for the newspapers and *The Bookman*. He was impudent, delighting in putting a thumb to his nose at tradition. He was better versed in the classics than *Vanity Fair* assumed him to be, but what really interested him was fresh and vivid contemporary work. He fought the battles of the young writers against the censors, and he avoided taking either himself or them too seriously.

Broun, in fact, did not take life seriously at all until he became aware of socialism, the labor movement, and the class struggle. His love for a fight, his hatred of injustice, and his natural sympathy for the underdog led him gradually from literary revolt to political rebellion. Largely abandoning literary and dramatic criticism, sports, and the numerous aspects of the contemporary scene which furnished topics for his *World* column, 'It Seems to Me,' he turned his attention almost entirely to the proletarian movement in politics, economics, and sociology. He marched with the garment-workers, carried placards, addressed mass meetings of strikers, and even joined the Socialist Party and ran, unsuccessfully, for Congress. The Socialist Party, for all its championship of independence of thought, imposes upon its members a rigid intellectual discipline. This was galling to the restless, individualistic Broun, and he withdrew from the party. He continues, however, his pinkish crusade, which at times takes on a Muscovite tinge of red.

Broun was one of a fairly large group of young men, most of them veterans of the war, who introduced vitality and liveliness into American journalism of the 'twenties. Other stars of the New York *World* included Harry Hansen, who began as the literary editor of the Chicago *Daily News* in 1920. On that interesting paper, where Carl Sandburg wrote editorials and Ben Hecht his *Thousand and One Afternoons in Chicago*, Hansen became the spokesman for the Chicago school of writers who, for a time, were the most vocal in the country. Hansen came to New York, as do so many Chicagoans when they become successful, and continued, on the *World* and later on the

World-Telegram and in *Harper's*, criticism which showed wide reading, a great familiarity with current and past literature, and little of the explosive disposition of Broun and Mencken.

Earlier Laurence Stallings, whose *Plumes* described his physically and spiritually tragic post-war experiences, contributed a column of smoothly written and rather bored criticism to the *World*. Returning from vacation in the fall of 1925, he complained wearily: 'One gets back to the reviewer's desk to understand again that the bulk of published stuff grows worse each season, just as ignorance flowers in direct proportion to the minority's enlargement of wisdom.' Stallings gave up criticism after his spectacular financial success on Broadway and in Hollywood, but for a while during the latter half of the decade he returned to the field to write long essays for the New York *Sun* which had little to do with the books he was supposed to be discussing.

RASCOE TWEAKS SOME EARS

STALLINGS greeted the newest batch of review copies with a yawn; Burton Rascoe pounced upon them with the enthusiasm of a child digging into his Christmas stocking. Rascoe, a Kentuckian who came to the New York *Tribune* from the Chicago *Tribune*, found books quite the most exciting things in the world, and he wrote about them with a combination of wonder, wide-eyed delight, and joy in inviting the public to share his pleasure with him. Rascoe had a wide acquaintance with the classics that was absent in most of his contemporary critics, but his reviews in the *Tribune* and *The Bookman* revealed an almost complete absorption in the books of the moment.

Equipped to talk about Petronius, Plutarch, or Dante with a Ph.D. of the campus, he was violently against the academicians. In Chicago his championing of Cabell before *Jurgen* made book-buyers conscious of him, and qualified Rascoe as a prophet and a protagonist of the new idea in literature. His 'Bookman's Daybook,' in which he recorded news of writers — such as Joseph Conrad's arrival in New York — bits of criticism, and vagrant notions about life and books, was for a while the most interesting literary column in America. Although written only once a week and largely confined to books, it had a newspaper circulation value that has no exact parallel in present-day journalism.

Rascoe, 'a smooth-faced, elegantly leggy lad,' to quote an anonymous sketch of him published in *The Bookman*, appeared to be in his early twenties when he was in his middle thirties. A good conversationalist, but modest and shy, he became an asset to parties in the decade in which writing men assumed greater social importance than they had ever before enjoyed in America. Meanness was as alien to him as reverence and respect for tradition. Once a friend tried to do him a grave injury. Rascoe heard about it, but when the friend wrote a book, Rascoe praised it warmly. Asked how he could have been so Christian, he replied simply that the book was a good book.

He became so well known as a person and a critic, in

what New Yorkers called 'the provinces' as well as in the city, that several publishers begged him to write a book. He promised, but the excitement of new publications and parties offered too great competition, and although publishers used every means short of the third degree, it was not until years later, when the literary excitement of the decade had subsided and his name was of definitely diminished box-office value, that he turned out *Titans of Literature* and *Prometheans.*

In his war against the academicians Rascoe had two favorite enemies, Brander Matthews and Stuart Sherman, the college professor who turned journalist. When Matthews in *The Tocsin of Revolt* proclaimed that the younger generation 'had never learned' how to write or paint and that their works were 'an exhalation of the lawless and the illegal, the illicit and the illegitimate,' Rascoe pounced on him by alleging that Matthews 'craves merely the privilege of age to indulge in such ancient mutterings,' and denounced him as one of the *gerontes* who did not understand or know what the new generation was trying to do.

A PROFESSOR RECANTS

SHERMAN was a worthier foe. The generalities of a Matthews were too easy for him, nor was he violent as was Lizette Woodworth Reese when she remarked simply that she would be glad to see the modern novelists hanged,

or Robert Herrick when he said of Ernest Hemingway's
A Farewell to Arms: 'It would not be too strong to call it
mere garbage.' Sherman was subtler. Moreover, he had
genuine learning, a greater degree of tolerance than many
of his adversaries who boasted of their tolerance, and a
firm kindness in criticism and controversy. Rascoe, as did
Mencken and the other new generation critics, found it
impossible to ridicule or blast him into silence. However
concerted and pointed the attack, he always returned to
the fray, fresh and bearing new weapons.

Sherman was teaching English literature to Middle-
Western college boys when Paul Elmer More, with the old
Nation, received some contributions from him which convinced him Sherman would make a capable protagonist of
traditionalism. The two exchanged much correspondence,
and, entering journalism as a protégé of More, Sherman
allied himself at once with the older generation in American
letters. Actually he was a year younger than Mencken,
Hergesheimer, and Van Vechten, two years younger than
Cabell, three years the junior of Sandburg, and five years
younger than Anderson. But when the younger generation stormed the parapets after the World War, they
saw in him an Elder who had to be demolished, and although he called *Main Street* the best novel of 1920 and
revered Mencken's idol, Walt Whitman, they kept up a
steady barrage against him and his ideas. Sherman did not
shrink from the fight, and he wrote clearly and effectively,
if not entertainingly. In a typical counterblast he said:

> In the busy hum of self-approbation which accompanies
> the critical activities of our 'young' people, perhaps the
> dominant note is their satisfaction at having emancipated

themselves from the fetters of tradition, the oppression of classical precedent and standard, the burden of a patrimonial culture. . . . It is relief to countless eager young souls that Mr. Mencken has dismissed all this as 'the fossil literature taught in colleges.' It is a joy to learn from Mr. Untermeyer that they may come out from the 'lifeless literary storehouse' and use life for their glossary, as indeed they may — or yesterday morning's newspaper.

To this mode of procuring a literary renascence there may be raised one objection: all experience is against it. . . .

Their novelists have lost a vision which Mr. Howells had: though they have shaken off the 'moralistic incubus' and have released their 'suppressed desires,' they have not learned to conceive or present a picture of civilized society.

Sherman often discovered the Achilles' heel of the younger generation. His attacks on the writers and the critics of the revolt annoyed, then enraged Rascoe; in the *Tribune* book pages Sherman appeared as a devil in cap and gown. It was ironical, therefore, when Sherman succeeded to Rascoe's job in 1924.

He did not, however, as many readers feared he would, bring with him into journalism a troupe of ancient, bearded, grim academicians from the college libraries. On the contrary, he gave the *Herald Tribune* a lively and interesting book section: Isabel Paterson, who probably has more to say than any other critic in New York today as to which books shall be popular and which shall be passed by, continued her amusing column of gossip which she calls 'Turns With a Bookworm,' and Irita Van Doren, now editor of the section, gave it a graceful and interesting makeup.

Sherman himself began to unbend. Perhaps he had

never been wholly on the side of those who first sponsored him and claimed him as their spokesman. Perhaps he had always felt that the younger generation possessed more merit than, in the heat of battle, he had admitted. At any rate, he gradually became interested in what the younger generation was doing. Novelty in ideas and form began to appeal to him; even Mencken in time came in for a few words of praise. By 1926, when his *Critical Woodcuts* appeared, a younger critic found he had broken 'through the cocoon of university thinking and come out strongly for the changing ideas and ideals of his time.' He died in October of that year, unwept alike by the Elders he had deserted and the younger generation into whose camp he had come uninvited.

ACADEMIC ATTACK ON YOUTH

SO FAR had Sherman progressed toward agreement with his one-time enemies that it is doubtful, had he lived, if he would have aligned with the Elders when, in 1928, they organized their philosophical and literary ideas into a 'movement.' By the time Irving Babbitt and Paul Elmer More, the founders of Humanism (as the movement was called, in imitation of an earlier one which restored Greek and Roman classics to vogue during the Renaissance), issued their manifesto, the Young Intellectuals had dissolved their lodge. The battle against censorship had been won. Most of the writers who had revolted so boisterously in the early part of the decade were silent or no longer interested in revolt. One rarely heard of the younger generation in literature. The post-war fever had subsided, and intellectual as well as social life at least approached the 'normalcy' which President Harding found to be the political need of the American people.

The time, then, was propitious for a counter-attack by the Elders. Not only were enemies fewer; in the normal course of events the cycle would be expected to produce conservatism in intellectual affairs, as in fashions it was soon to cover the feminine knee, which for so long had been on public view.

The movement appeared in the first month of 1928, when *The Forum* declared war on Mencken, 'the facile penman of *The American Mercury*,' and called for the emergence of 'another school of critics in America whose skepticism resembles that of Montaigne, in that they doubt out of a greater faith.' Waiting in the wings for this call were More, Babbitt, Sherlock Bronson Gass, a professor of rhetoric at the University of Nebraska, and Norman Foerster of the University of North Carolina. With a small group of cohorts, they stepped quickly to the center of the stage, and for a few months Humanism ranked almost with Radio Common as a topic of conversation.

It is interesting to note that, like the terms 'Puritanism' and 'Victorianism' as they were used in the early part of the decade, Humanism eludes precise definition. The newest edition of *Webster's New International Dictionary* describes the movement as a belief in the perfectibility of man, a religious conception which substitutes faith in man for faith in God. But its high priests were unable to agree upon so simple a statement of their creed. To More, Humanism was 'a moral law of character.' To Babbitt, it was 'a standard set above temperament.' To Gass, it was a realization 'that the central problem, and hence the central interest, of life — since life and intelligence are given — is what to make of it, that is, what values to pursue in it.'

T. S. Eliot, who produced in 1922 a long and widely debated poem called 'The Waste Land' which became the literary sensation of the year, further complicated the matter. Eliot had joined the Anglo-Catholic Church, and toward the latter half of the decade became more and more preoccupied with religion, as his volume of verse, *Ash Wednesday*, reveals. Eliot wanted Humanism to embrace the mysticism and poetry of Mother Church, and though More and Babbitt never formally admitted the religious theme, Eliot was an authentic Humanist. Michael Williams, the brilliant editor of the Catholic magazine, *The Commonweal*, grasped the opportunity to argue that American literature 'must follow the lead of certain neo-Catholic tendencies in European letters and return to religion,' but he, too, failed to get a religious plank in the platform.

The Humanists, in fact, were wary of all attempts to define their movement. One convert argued the virtues of Humanism through book reviews in a Southern paper. When the columnist on the same book page called on him for a brief definition of the movement, arguing that any

intelligible idea could be defined in fifty words, Seward
Collins, who had bought *The Bookman* and turned it into a
Humanist organ, hastily wrote the young Humanist warn-
ing him against the perils of committing himself.

Whether Humanism was primarily religious, moral, or
literary, it was definitely a movement of the professors.
Its leaders were men of a vast amount of book learning,
with a deep respect for the judgments and standards of the
past. They were not journalistic in their writings, which
means, briefly, that they were not principally concerned
with being entertaining. They did not write for the newspapers and the literary supplements, but for the learned
reviews. They rejected the great body of American literature as lacking the broad philosophical background which
they believed to be necessary to great novels, and they
rejected American criticism as being facile, directionless,
and superficial. They were, in brief, against all that was
'modern' in American letters, against all the tenets of the
younger generation.

More divided the modern writers into two schools —
the 'esthetic,' as represented by Cabell and Amy Lowell,
and the 'realistic,' as exemplified by Dreiser, Anderson,
Edgar Lee Masters, and Lewis. The former, he said, make
'a divorce between the true in life and the beautiful in art
which must spell death to any serious emotion in literature,' while the realists are not sufficiently educated, but
'self-made men with no inherited background of culture.'
Of Dreiser, the realist who came nearest to getting their
imprimatur, More wrote:

> If only he knew the finer aspects of life as he knows its
> shabby underside; if only his imagination had been trained

in the larger tradition of literature instead of getting its
bent from the police court and the dregs of science; if only
religion had appeared to him in other garb than the trav-
esty of superstition and faded fanaticism; if only he had
had a chance, he might possibly have produced that
fabulous thing, the great American novel.

For a while, the Humanists were fairly belligerent.
They wrote well, if not as brightly as many of their
enemies, and they combined a barrage against the young
with a confident assumption that they alone were equipped
to set the intellectual and moral standards of America.
The Bookman gave them a mouthpiece for their ideas and,
more importantly, a medium through which they could
appraise current literature according to Humanist standards and thus exert an influence on contemporary writing.
They showed a boldness that seemed for a while to promise
an exciting controversy. Babbitt, writing in *The Forum* of
February, 1928, chose as his enemy the most brilliant and
resourceful champion of the younger generation. What
America had needed, he said, was a Socrates, and it got a
Mencken. 'The characteristic evils of the present age arise
from unrestraint and violation of the law of measure and
not, as our modernists would have us believe, from the
tyranny of taboos and traditional inhibitions.'

THE COUNTER-RAID

THIS was a frontal attack on the principles dearest to the younger generation, and a group of them quickly reassembled to put the heresy down. Under the editorship of C. Hartley Grattan they produced a volume called *The Critique of Humanism* as a reply to *Humanism and America.* In it they attacked every facet of the movement. Grattan exposed its philosophical poverty; Edmund Wilson dissected a few of the Humanist ideas; Henry Hazlitt argued that their thinking was muddled; Allen Tate discovered that they, too, were without direction or design; and Burton Rascoe subjected them to a psychoanalysis intended to make them seem silly.

Mencken, who had lambasted More and Babbitt for years, was delighted when they gave him a tangible target, and he belabored them with the delight of an adolescent wielding a paddle at a fraternity initiation. Noting that the movement was getting some attention on the campuses where a few years before he had reigned supreme, he wrote:

> It is their very feebleness, of course, that makes them popular among certain varieties of sophomores, both in and out of college. They give comfort to youngsters who might otherwise suffer damnably, confronting a skeptical and ribald world. These youngsters are the sons of Babbitts and are doomed to go through life as Babbitts themselves. But when they get to college and begin to read forbidden books they make the disconcerting discovery that most of the values they have been brought up to re-

vere are widely questioned, and by men who appear to be
well regarded. Their dismay may seem comical to the
spectator, but to them it is agony. I believe that Humanism, like its brother, Rotarianism, relieves that agony
effectively, and is thus worthy of the support of all humane
men. It convinces them that, after all, the pastor back
home is probably right — that papa, running his sash-
weight factory, is really a better man than Cabell or
Dreiser — that the United States sought no profit in the
late war — that the editorials in the *Saturday Evening
Post* are profound — that Sacco and Vanzetti, being wops,
got only what was coming to them. Thus convinced, they
proceed to their destiny with glad hearts, and are naturally
grateful to their deliverers.

Humanism never was the same after the Grattan symposium. The younger generation had shown that, though
they were scattered and less belligerent than they were in
the early years of the decade, they were determined to
preserve what they had won, and that they were willing to
do battle to preserve it. Against their brilliance and
journalistic skill, against their superior numbers, the
Humanists were helpless.

The Humanists labored under self-imposed as well as
inherent handicaps. They had restricted themselves to a
formula, and thus could not employ the unconventional
strategy of their swashbuckling opponents. They were
naturally cautious. They were accustomed to writing for
men of learning, and when the time came to present their
ideas vigorously and attractively to the masses, they were
unequal to the occasion. Their attitude of exclusiveness —
they rejected practically the entire body of American
literature save the books of Babbitt, the tracts of More,
and Dorothy Canfield's novel *The Brimming Cup* — in-

evitably seemed strained. In general, they seemed of, by, and for the classroom. And so Humanism by the end of the decade was almost forgotten — never mentioned in the magazines or newspapers, and recalled by only a few critics as a somewhat gallant but futile counter-raid by the Elders upon the forts from which the Younger Generation had driven them when *This Side of Paradise*, *Jurgen*, and *Main Street* scattered them in confusion.

In the field of criticism, then, the moderns still were the victors. Grown a little more tolerant with the years, less sure of themselves now that middle age was upon them or just around the corner, a little less noisy and excitable, they kept their standard waving. Freshness and novelty were no longer the highest desideratum in writing, but they were still welcome. To be shocking was not enough, though the writer could be shocking if he wished. Books continued to be judged without reference to a textbook conception of technique. The books that were praised were those which made an honest attempt to portray the realities of life, and it did not matter whether the author presented the 'shabby underside' or Park Avenue, whether he had got his training in the police courts or from 'the larger tradition of literature.' And in this defeat of the Humanists, the younger generation in criticism demonstrated that they were not merely a fad, a product of special social and intellectual conditions. For better or worse, they had diverted the stream of American criticism into a new channel.

VI. THE VOGUE FOR VOGUES

VI. THE VOGUE FOR VOGUES

> One of the striking characteristics of the era of Coolidge
> Prosperity was the unparalleled rapidity and unanimity
> with which millions of men and women turned their
> attention, their talk, and their emotional interest upon a
> series of tremendous trifles.
>
> FREDERICK LEWIS ALLEN: *Only Yesterday*

NINETEEN–TWENTY to 1930 was the decade of 'normalcy,' the Florida boom, the Teapot Dome scandals, the Big Bull Market, prohibition, and an astonishingly successful revolution in manners. It was also a decade of fads. The war generation had started to play and needed continual shots of Something New to keep its mind from those years when life had been so fast, fierce, and occasionally so tragic. It got the Charleston, Coué, mah jong, Gertrude Stein, golf, Greta Garbo, crossword puzzles, and spiritualism.

This craze for crazes created the faddist, who exercised his talents for modernity by assiduously keeping up with and popularizing 'the latest thing,' and if possible, by inventing today what would be tomorrow's 'latest thing.' A famous faddist was Carl Van Vechten, who possessed an astounding range of interests for a literary man and enough enthusiasm to spread generously over the lot.

Anything that was being talked about intrigued Van Vechten. He urged *The Richmond Reviewer* to print a piece of Gertrude Stein's before notice of that lady's importance had more than trickled back from Paris, and when the American public still expected words to fit together with some semblance of sense. *The Reviewer* took his advice and used an article starting, 'One little Indian boy, two little Indian boy, three little Indian boy, four little Indian boy, five little Indian boy, six little Indian boy' — and so on in conclusive proof that Miss Stein knew how to count. (This was titled, appropriately enough, 'Indian Boy.') Later the same magazine printed an appreciation of Van Vechten by Miss Stein, and he was forced to confess he had no idea what it meant.

Van Vechten exhumed Edgar Saltus and Henry Fuller, two interesting writers who had received little popular acclaim. He succeeded with Saltus, in the case of *Historia Amoris* and *The Imperial Orgy*. But he made little headway with Fuller's promotion, on which he had distinguished aid — James Huneker had called him master, and Agnes Repplier and William Dean Howells and others had praised him highly. Although Van Vechten announced that *The Last Refuge* was 'a forerunner of *South Wind* and quite comparable to that book in its degree of glamor,' the public remained apathetic to Fuller's tales of Italy and modern Chicago. Ronald Firbank, an airily sophisticated Englishman, was imported by Van Vechten, who insisted he would soon develop into a great talent. Firbank died, however, before this promise was fulfilled, and left only a few novels — *Prancing Nigger* was the best.

In a lull between literary fads Van Vechten took up the Charleston. The white-haired, middle-aged dilettante

Acme

THE CHARLESTON
Carl Van Vechten wanted to teach a class

Acme

DARK ART
Harlem hi-de-ho was popularized by writers of the 'twenties

even considered instructing a class in the rowdiest and most strenuous dance the ballroom had ever seen. He then discovered Harlem, when the cabarets and night clubs of that district were not patronized by white persons, and shortly Harlem was the smart place to go dancing. As a musical critic of standing (he practiced criticism for twenty years) he was enthusiastic about modern music. He acclaimed Stravinsky when most Americans considered the latter's work merely clashing noise, and joined with Gilbert Seldes in panegyrics of George Gershwin. Although his interests were scattered, he was capable of thorough work on certain subjects. *The Tiger in the House*, a gracefully written defense of cats, represents an awe-inspiring amount of research in European and American libraries.

DARK ART

VAN VECHTEN was an unofficial press-agent for the Negro Renaissance, which attracted an enormous amount of attention in the first half of the 'twenties. The Young Intellectuals were demonstrating their lack of race prejudice by vociferous praise of the art of the down-trodden black brother. White critics as well welcomed the writings of Negroes with gratifying hospitality, and white authors wrote almost as many books about Negroes as the blacks wrote about themselves. There were Herbert Seligmann's *The Negro Faces America*, Carl Sandburg's *The Chicago Race Riots*, T. S. Stribling's *Birthright*, Irvin Cobb's *J. Poindexter, Colored*, H. A. Shands's *White and Black*, and the burlesque stories of Octavus Roy Cohen and E. K. Means. Eugene O'Neill, Du Bose Heyward, Julia Peterkin, and Ridgely Torrence brought the race into prominence on the stage with *All God's Chillun Got Wings*, *Porgy*, *Green Thursday*, and *Granny Maumee*.

The Negroes themselves produced copiously. As early in the decade as 1922 Paul Laurence Dunbar's *Complete Poems* had appeared, James Weldon Johnson's *Fifty Years*, Joseph S. Cotter's *The Bank of Gideon*, William Holtzclaw's *The Black Man's Burden*, Robert Moton's *Finding a Way Out*, *The Book of American Negro Poetry*, edited by Johnson, Claude McKay's *Harlem Shadows*, and *Darkwater* by W. E. B. Du Bois, who later appeared in the *Encyclopaedia Britannica*, writing on Negro literature.

But although they wrote prolifically and some of them wrote skillfully, the worth of their literature may be questioned now the fad has died. That they used their art as a channel of race propaganda is now fairly obvious, and, although no one in the 'twenties seemed disturbed by this, it resulted in a lopsided literature, some of it as inartistic as any sociological treatise. Few of the Negro writers and poets resisted the temptation to state the case of their race while the whites were welcoming their work so kindly. Walter White, prominent in the movement, wrote *Fire in the Flint*, which turned out to be a sort of *Uncle Tom's Cabin* of modern days, treating violently of

Southern wrongs. The admired Countée Cullen, so vehement an objector to Negro propaganda in literature, admitted that 'somehow or other ... I find my poetry of itself treating of the Negro.' Even Du Bois's *Gift of the Black Folk* and *The New Negro*, edited by Alain Locke, the best of the non-fiction lot, were full of the social-problem attitude.

Worse, they now expected the same treatment from white writers. So the reverberation was terrific when Van Vechten abandoned fads and too-facile fiction to produce his serious novel, *Nigger Heaven*. It treated Harlem realistically, and its characters were set forth as humans instead of perambulating problems. Harlem did not care for this at all, and although Van Vechten's best novel gave the race tremendous sympathy and under-standing, it was regarded there as a *faux pas*.

Nigger Heaven appeared in 1926, and though the book probably had little to do with it, the vogue for Negro literature began to decline around that date. The sub-ject of the 'Renaissance' grew wearisome; too much en-thusiasm had worn it out. Critics sincerely interested in Negroes and their writings did the objects of their ad-miration a disservice by noisy applause, and by turning what might have been a strong movement into a fad, postponed a real renascence indefinitely.

FOR EVERY FAD A LIBRARY

NEGRO literature, even at the top of its popularity, did not hold the fad arena unchallenged; there were enough contenders to confuse any country but America. The sensational 'twenties produced them so rapidly that it was difficult for moderns to keep their dinner conversation up to date. War books and books on psychic phenomena were the first of the literary 'rages.' The former occupied a big percentage of space in the book stalls in 1919 and 1920; in 1919 of fifty novels of any claim to worth thirty dealt with the World War. Nearly all were disgustingly sentimental and false — so much so that John Dos Passos's realistic *Three Soldiers* received a New York *Times* review concluding with the remark that it was easy to understand why the dust jacket was yellow.

The psychic phenomena fad was as direct a product of the war. The possibility of communication with sons, brothers, and sweethearts killed at the front caused it to be an instant success, and America seized trustingly on the writings of Arthur Conan Doyle and Oliver Lodge and their many imitators. Some of these books were sincere, some 'phoney,' nearly all ridiculous. A Mrs. Percy Drearmer alleged that she collaborated with a literary spirit who did the writing while she looked out of the window or sewed — thus *The Fellowship of the Picture* was produced. Mack Stauffer said the material for *Humanity and the Mysterious Knight* came to him in

a series of hazy dreams. Similar idiocies permeated painting. One Prince Childe de Rohan-d'Harcourt, 'the
mystic poet-painter of the unseen,' exhibited an astral
portrait of President Harding and gave a little talk for
the ladies on 'How President Warren G. Harding Came
to See Me After His Death.'

While the reading public was awed at the prophecies
of ouija boards, a medium figured in a novel of Robert
Hichens. Other fiction-writers made profitable use of the
trappings of spiritualism, *séances* full of floating tables,
voices from the unknown, and misty spectral faces. In
the meantime all-too-real mediums wandered over the
country, pocketing large sums from credulous persons,
chiefly women. The absurdity was not to go undebated,
and there were a few books attacking the psychic fad.
But America refused to relinquish her plaything until
she was tired of it, and no one paid much attention to
the dissenters or their writings.

By 1923 this foolishness had been laid to rest and
people were talking of Mary Garden, the Ziegfeld Follies,
Einstein, fireless cookers, the Russian Ballet, Charlie
Chaplin, *The Little Review*, the tango, Marcel Proust,
Dadaism, glands, mah jong, and Coué. Particularly were
they talking of M. Émile Coué, who offered a phrase —
'Every day, in every way, I'm getting better and better'
— as a cure for all ills.

While Coué possibly was saying to himself, Every day
in every way, my book is selling better and better,' upon
the best-seller list with his *Self-Mastery* were H. G. Wells's
Outline of History and *The Outline of Science* by J. Arthur
Thomson, and only a few steps down were Hendrik Van

Loon's *Story of Mankind* and *Outwitting Our Nerves* by Jackson and Salisbury. The decade of tired business men, nervous breakdowns, phobias, and jitters called out many panaceas of the type of *Outwitting Our Nerves*, and produced the credulous state of mind which made possible the swallowing of such ludicrous theories as Coué's. Coué, incidentally, did not confine himself to such relatively simple ailments, promising cure for club feet, asthma, frontal sinus, and humps.

While toying with the fascinating subject of nerves and mental healing America was catching short ones of culture from hefty kegs put on the market by Wells, Van Loon, and numerous learned authors who had crammed an astonishing amount of knowledge into their omnibus products. The public read outlines of science, literature, art, ethics, civilization, and Einstein, and would have become able to discourse brilliantly on Pasteur, Shaw, Monet, Aristotle, Why Rome Fell, or Relativity, if the information had not been assimilated in shockingly muddled form. The outline authors, of course, did not write their books to raise the cultural standards of the masses, but they must have been disturbed by the confusion into which they plunged uninformed minds. Certainly Will Durant, who popularized with his *Story of Philosophy* a subject that should have remained unpopularized, had a dubious effect on college papers. A professor reports he received this from a formerly bored pupil: 'Now we come to good old Schope, cheerful beggar that he was.'

Nearly all the fads of the 'twenties had literary ramifications. Authorities on golf sprang up as American business men discovered that plus-fours had a certain sportiness and that many brief-skirted girls were to be found traversing the courses (the golf widow was an early 'twenties phenomenon only). These experts fought pen battles over the difference of one-half inch in a putting stance, and the public, open-mindedly enough, was eager to read the many controversial answers to such questions. It was the same with bridge, although contract had yet to put in an appearance and complicate matters another several hundred books' worth. And although mah jong was one of the most fleeting of the epidemics there was time for the experts to get into print months before the craze collapsed. Radio, too, regarded in the early days with such awe and loving admiration, was the inspiration for many treatises on the intricacies of tubes and advice on what to do when the outside aerial blew down.

In spite of the Reverend John Roach Straton's thunderings against the drinking party, that new American institution did not consist solely of contests to see who could get around the most gin, 'lascivious dancing,' and infidelities in the garden. It did in part, but the post-war craving for 'something to do' was so strong that other entertainment had to be provided. So question books and guggenheim books came into being, and *What's the Answer? Guess Again*, *What's Your Average?* and many others became necessary accessories to a hostess's equipment. Fully as popular were crossword puzzles and numerology, both calling forth their quota of books.

The former, incidentally, helped launch the publishing house of Simon and Schuster in 1924. Crossword puzzles had been appearing in a few newspapers, but no one had ever brought out a book of them. A relative of Richard Simon's expressed a desire for such a book. After thinking the matter over, Simon played his hunch, and by the end of the decade the total sales of Simon and Schuster's *Cross-Word Puzzle Book* had passed the two-million mark.

'GHOSTS' AND DEBUNKERS

DURING the 'twenties the dailies and magazines were filled with signed articles by such professional sportsmen as George Hermann Ruth, Jack Dempsey, and Louis Angel Firpo. The public read and believed and remarked on how nice it was that baseball players and pugilists were so handy with the written word. Ghost-writing rose to be a profession. It became fashionable for financiers to hire 'ghosts' to write their autobiographies. Ghost-writers out of work invaded penitentiaries to get the life stories of prominent criminals, and the results, embroidered with lurid details, would nearly always be published in book form or at least sold for goodly sums to tabloids for serial purposes. *Doomed Ship* by Judd Gray, a leading character in the famous Gray-Snyder murder case, received such favorable reviews that several prominent New York ghosts claimed authorship.

There grew up in the 'twenties a cult of debunkers, whose purpose was to slash away the underbrush of sentiment surrounding great historical figures and to present biographies of human beings, not copy-book heroes. Thomas Beer 'exposed' a period in *The Mauve Decade* and received for this adroit and careful piece of work the profits of debunking and those realized by anyone who could make the Victorian way of life look silly. His was probably the most famous of the debunking books, but the phrase was invented by W. E. Woodward, who came to rue the day he thought of it, fearing *Meet General Grant* and his other new-formula biographies would be subordinated in importance to the word he contributed to the American language.

Woodward's books and the books of a few other debunkers were well written and documented with reasonable care, but many of his followers 'exposed' their way to absurdity, invariably placing the most damaging interpretation on the facts.

DIKRAN AND ANITA

THERE were cases of excessive popularity, too fleeting to be anything but fads. Dikran Kuymjian, an Armenian known to his British and American public as Michael Arlen, was an urbane, mustached little man, always to be seen at the correct British and Riviera resorts at the correct seasons, dressed in the most impeccably correct clothes. He wrote of a mythical English society, gentlemen overweighted with honor and women with names like Shelmerdene and Diavalen. This nobility was excessively glamorous and excessively adulterous, but the Armenian presented his material so charmingly that the reader seldom realized what ridiculous stuff he was enjoying. When *The Green Hat* was published in America *The London Venture*, *The Romantic Lady*, *These Charming People*, and *Piracy* appeared too, but *The Green Hat* was enough to turn Arlen into an emblem of sophisticated naughtiness and urbanity.

Another one-man fad, or in this case a one-woman fad, was Anita Loos, who wrote *Gentlemen Prefer Blondes*. This *Illuminating Diary of a Professional Lady* was written by a pert-looking little person with shaggy hair and reportorial instincts who had been working in Hollywood, where she observed models for Lorelei and her Mr. Gus Eisman, the Button King. Straight from the film capital, the author enjoyed herself tremendously when an amazed and delighted public wondered if the book had been written in all naïveté. She was amused and enriched when chorus girls, manicurists, and other professional ladies bought it under the impression that it would give them further insight into the intricacies of the male mind.

But everybody loved *Gentlemen Prefer Blondes*, no matter why they read it. Mencken remarked that it was 'full of shrewd observation and devastating irony,' and Van Vechten went on record with 'It ranks as a work of art.' Other people said, more simply, that it was swell, and made a point of attending the stage version to hear Dorothy make her famous observation to the effect that a kiss on the hand is fine but a diamond bracelet lasts longer. The production of this small amount of wordage — the book is about the length of James Hilton's *Goodbye, Mr. Chips* — made Miss Loos.

She wrote articles as an expert on female ice-hunters, and her personable little figure was garbed by Parisian couturiers and photographed for fashion magazines. Her book sold and sold, and so she wrote another. It sold too, its wheels oiled by the success of the first, but the freshness of the idea had worn off and it received comparatively little attention. Miss Loos as a literary fad finally went the way of Coué and the question books, the same general direction already taken by Michael Arlen.

But while the public was applauding the Loos literature it was almost as important to procure a first edition of *Gentlemen Prefer Blondes* as it was to have 'first printing' on the fly leaf of one's copies of *Main Street* and *A Story Teller's Story*. The country had gone first-edition mad, and, for the first time, contemporary American literature was considered the most valuable thing to collect. Second-hand bookshops were searched for any firsts available, though the preferred authors were Anderson, Cabell, Dreiser, Lewis, Cather, Van Vechten, Wharton, Glasgow, Hemingway, Hergesheimer, Fitzgerald. Bookshop proprietors promoted the fad by running up prices far above previous sums received for contemporary work. Publishers sent to literary editors announcements of new books long before these were to be published, and the news would appear in book columns in plenty of time for enthusiasts to get in early orders at the stores. Thus firsts were usually sold before publication, though publishers ran off huge initial editions.

For wealthier book-lovers limited editions held even more appeal. Beautifully printed and illustrated books, with 'type distributed' printed on the last page, were bought up almost immediately on publication and frequently before. Cabell was the collectors' favorite during the book boom, and there are many homes inhabited by persons who have never read his books where one can find editions *de luxe* of *The Way of Ecben*, *The High Place*, *The Music From Behind the Moon*, *The Silver Stallion*, *Jurgen*, *The White Robe*. The higher the price the faster limited editions sold, and fifteen or twenty dollars for a book was considered not at all unreasonable. People bought and bought, expecting the ever-rising book market to continue to rise indefinitely. But the bottom fell out with the depression, and amateur collectors hard pressed for cash have found their libraries will not bring even one fourth of the original investment.

Gilbert Seldes crystallized with *The Seven Lively Arts* some of the current pets of the *cognoscenti* whose business it was to bestow their admiration on non-academic phases of art and literature. The intellectuals pored over the comic strip of George Herriman's angular Krazy Kat, and analyzed at length the 'feeling' in Charlie Chaplin's feet. John Alden Carpenter composed a Krazy Kat ballet which was briefly the talk of New York. Charlie Chaplin became Charles Chaplin in '21, as Frank Crowninshield, editor of *Vanity Fair*, guided him through the doors of New York society. When on a trip to England Chaplin remarked he liked to read Anatole France in bed, large pictures of the French sage made the front pages of English dailies. The actor, however, was so misguided as to write *My Trip Abroad*, whereupon the critics advised him to confine his activities to the screen.

Milt Gross, the prodigy out of the Bronx, was another thinkers' delight, with his *Dunt Esk* and *Nize Baby* experiments in East Side speech. Another was E. E. Cummings (e. e. cummings, as he writes it), who wrote this program note for the production of his bizarre play *Him* at the Provincetown Theater in 1928:

> WARNING: him isn't a comedy or a tragedy or a farce or a melodrama or a revue or an operetta or a moving picture or any other convenient excuse for 'going to the theater' — in fact it's a PLAY, so let it PLAY; and because you are here, let it PLAY with you. . . . Relax, and give this PLAY a chance to strut its stuff — relax, don't worry because it's not like something else — relax, stop wondering what it's all 'about' — like many strange and familiar things, Life included, this PLAY isn't 'about,' it simply is. Don't try to despise it, let it try to despise you. Don't try to enjoy it, let it try to enjoy you. DON'T TRY TO UNDERSTAND IT, LET IT TRY TO UNDERSTAND YOU.

DOWN WITH SEX SUPPRESSION

THE young intellectuals interested in personal and particularly amorous freedom, in the middle of the decade turned their attention to a voice from Denver. Judge Ben B. Lindsey, well known as a sympathetic arbiter on the juvenile bench, took a look at the marital difficulties of the times and found them soluble only by companionate marriage. He wrote *The Companionate Marriage*, which for an innocuous and sensible book created a frightful storm.

Lindsey's plan, as he outlined it, was simply this: the practice of legalized birth control by parties to a marriage, the divorce of childless couples by mutual consent, and the lack of financial or economic claim by either party upon the other. In a sexy decade, surely this was not revolutionary. It was, in fact, almost old-fashioned. But somehow, probably through the angry rantings and misinterpretations of churchmen and conservatives, it became heralded that Judge Lindsey was advocating non-legal unions, dissoluble at any time whether the couple was childless or not and by either party and for the most trivial of reasons. Young rebels thought this a sound marital system, and lent their cheers to a cause to which they would have been indifferent had they troubled to read Lindsey's book.

The Companionate Marriage did have a fat sale, though, which was egged on by pulpit denunciations. The Elders had been grieving over the breakup in morals since the beginning of the decade. People expected marriage to become obsolete as they expected the family system to dodder and die, and it was typical of a period wherein things occurred so quickly that they foresaw these events as happening overnight. The shocking undress of women, bawdy talk in polite conversation, heavy consumption of bootleg whiskey, the restlessness and unconventionality that blazed from the young people, all descended on heretofore puritanical America in a flash, wherefore it was natural to suppose that the institution of marriage would disappear from the American scene as suddenly as had 'limbs,' and good liquor.

Alarmists who read Judge Lindsey's book predicted an even quicker demise. Publicity exploded over Lindsey's head, and for a while he was the most talked-of man in America. Publicity fell, too, on a few persons who announced to reporters that they were entering into companionate marriages; among these was the son of E. Haldeman-Julius.

Because Bertrand Russell's *Marriage and Morals* appeared much later in the 'twenties, when it was harder to get a rise out of the Elders, that book caused little excitement from the moralistic point of view. It certainly contained more inflammable material than Lindsey's. Russell argued that marriage is a much healthier institution if both parties take the liberty of wandering into amorous bypaths when they so desire. He deplored abstinence from extra-marital affairs as much as furtiveness in conducting such affairs, and visualized a superhumanly tolerant and sane race of men and women should society be organized along the lines he suggested. The Englishman's obviously fine mind lent added interest to the persons of intellectual pretensions who subscribed to his ideas; they were somewhat dashed at the news of Russell's recent divorce, during which it was revealed that he and his wife had found mutual infidelity unsatisfactory.

Russell and Lindsey were food for the young immorals, but Freud was their stiff drink. He did not specify how infidelities should be managed, but stated that suppression of the sex impulse must be avoided. It caused numberless perversions, dread complexes, and awful phobias. Suppression came to mean all that was horrible in human conduct; an agile-minded psychiatrist could trace to it a murder or a dislike of spinach. Many young men and women, shocked at what they considered the indecent restraint of their parents' lives, readily accepted invitations to each others' beds. Virgins, of either sex, were curiosities, to be weightily argued over and discussed by their friends — for this was an era when everyone told the world of his sexual affairs.

While it was thus becoming reactionary to sleep with the same person for as many nights as there are in a week, Freud's books and interpretations of his books were rolling from the presses as rapidly as they could be printed, and a new type of biography, the psychoanalytical, rivaled the books of the debunkers.

THE LAST BOHEMIA

GREENWICH VILLAGE had more Freudians than tea shops. America's Montmartre had had a reputation for free love since the days when artists and writers first discovered it was a cheap and charming place to live, but with the advent of the 'twenties and Freud, sin and the Village became synonymous in the minds of good citizens. Ménages rearranged themselves so rapidly that the stock greeting could have been, 'Hello, who are you living with this week?' Couples so misguided as to wed took elaborate pains to conceal that fact. Landlords began to worry when forces for morality displayed an ominous activity, and they issued this plea in the New York *Times*: 'We do not like the reputation of being an artists' quarter where abandon is expected and condoned. We want real people here and real artists and professional people, not those who sojourn here because they think this is a place where anything goes.'

Whether the landlords got many 'real people' in the gaudy 'twenties is doubtful. It is said Noel Coward was one of the hungry inhabitants early in the decade, but soon after he was appeasing his appetite with caviar as the idol of London and, later, New York. Edna St. Vincent Millay, after being pronounced the younger generation's poet because of *A Few Figs From Thistles*, did the unmentionable and married, retreating to a rural life in the Adirondacks. Willa Cather lived in the Village awhile, giving well-known and entertaining Friday afternoon teas. Eugene O'Neill did some of his best work there, in the days before he hoaxed the intelligentsia with such pretentiousness as *Strange Interlude*. But shortly after the decade opened nearly every literary person who has been heard from since had abandoned what has been called the world's last Bohemia. Gone were the good old days when the waiters argued the virtues of *vers libre* with the customers; when the 'pagan routs' at Webster Hall were almost worthy of this tag Floyd Dell had found in the thesaurus for them; when Dreiser would play 'Up Jenkins' with a crowd of Villagers until dawn came through the restaurant windows; when Sherwood Anderson took a minor part in the theatrical production, minus scenery, costumes, and funds, which marked the birth of the Little Theater movement in New York; when around *The Masses* grouped John Reed, George Bellows, Louis Untermeyer, Mary Vorse, Horatio Winslow, Howard Brubaker, John Sloan, and Floyd Dell, all delighting in the frequent suppressions granted the magazine by the postal authorities.

The old ways and the old people were chased away when uptowners got wind of naughty doings among the intellectuals living below Fourteenth Street, and descended on the Village in sight-seeing droves in search of sin. It was not uncommon for these aliens to appear in restaurants, introduce themselves to a party of Villagers, and ask to be shown the sights, magnanimously offering to pay all expenses. Dell describes his writhings when pointed out to a gaping group as a 'typical Villager.'

Real estate men helped to vanquish the Village aborigines. The invaders were willing to pay for picturesqueness, so rents jumped from twenty-five dollars a month to a hundred and twenty-five; and for those who desired their atmosphere in comfort large apartment-houses were built, equipped with all the uptown accessories such as florist shops, drugstores, and expensive restaurants. A host of small eating, drinking, and dance places catered to tourists: the Pepper Pot, the Mad Hatter, the Pig and Whistle Inn in Ye Olde Greenwich Village, the Green Witch, La Bohème, the Jolly Friars Inn, the Moulin Rouge Cave, the Cricket, and the Flamingo. The Pirate's Den, in Christopher Street, boasted 'Red George,' who

POET AS AUCTIONEER

Maxwell Bodenheim hawks the verse of Norma Keating at the
annual poetry exhibit in the Village

appeared in tattered boots, and with a knife between the teeth and hair pulled over his eyes went about his business of giving women customers a pleasant little fright. Professional Villagers haunted these places; one, dressed romantically in velvet coat and wide hat, sold candies — 'the color of your psyche, dear lady.'

Obviously little work of value could flourish in such a fraudulently Bohemian atmosphere. Robert Edwards, one of the moving spirits of the place and editor of *The Quill*, the only Village magazine to live through the decade, admitted:

> If your verse is very vile
> You might send it to *The Dial*.
> If your verse is viler still —
> Send, oh, send it to *The Quill*.

Mencken disposed of the *literati* below Washington Square with

> The Village produces nothing that justifies all the noise it makes. I have yet to hear of a first-rate book coming out of it, or a short story of arresting quality, or even a poem of solid distinction.... It is, in the overwhelming main, jejune and imitative. The prose is quite without distinction, either in matter or in manner. The verse seldom gets beyond a hollow audaciousness, not unlike that of cubist painting. It is not often, indeed, that even personality is in it; all of the Villagers seem to write alike.

To Villagers, however, Mencken was as reactionary as any professor, and his condemnation could not have fluttered them. They were a snobbish lot. Frank Shay, bookshop proprietor and editor of the weekly, *The Greenwich Villager*, snootily defined the lure of the section: 'In all this great United States it is the only place a person can sport a stocking with a hole in the heel, and an idea. Elsewhere both are taboo.'

Discussions of 'art' became endless, eccentricities more self-conscious. Everyone sidestepped hard work in favor of talk about it, in revolt against the middle-class motto that time is money. A writers' club was launched and the weekly luncheons were eaten in reverse order, dessert first, because the bourgeoisie are conformists enough to begin with soup. There was discussion of printing magazine pieces upside down because the *Saturday Evening Post* and *Cosmopolitan* printed theirs right side up. In the 'hydraulic issue' of Jane Gooch's *Vortex* photographs of washbasins at different angles were compared to work of Michelangelo. Miss Gooch said representations of rubber bath sponges and soap would be laughed at, 'but we're used to that, and if anything is going to be done to bring the American public to a real appreciation of art... it will have to be done in the teeth of the sneers and ridicule of all the kept art critics of the bourgeois magazines.' Chet Keppel, 'metaphysical poet' and Greenwich Village prophet, was jailed for stealing furs, which in a Robin-Hood-like frame of mind he gave to the poor.

Those who lived there said the chief charm of the Village was its lack of commercial feeling, but young men and women who had gathered from Chicago, San Francisco, Peoria, and Paducah and taken refuge in lower New York to escape the big-business ideal of America ran antique shops, bookshops, bridge parlors, dance-halls, night clubs, real estate offices, and tea shops. Groups found it advantageous to patronize regularly certain speakeasies; materialistic proprietors served up free drinks to weirdly dressed customers so easily recognized as Villagers by the uptown patrons.

Greenwich Village did not become a fad until the 'twenties, when by too much self-publicizing it walked voluntarily to a literary grave, where it lay down and immediately expired, leaving real estate agents, 'red ink' vendors, and tea shop proprietors to romp away with the profits, and spurious writers to commit assault and battery upon a once fine artistic reputation.

VII. PAYMENT IN FAME

VII. PAYMENT IN FAME

Then a sentimental passion of a vegetable fashion
Must excite your languid spleen,
An attachment à *la* Plato for a bashful young potato,
Or a not-too-French French bean!
Though the Philistines may jostle, you will rank as an
    apostle
In the high esthetic band,
If you walk down Piccadilly with a poppy or a lily
In your medieval hand.

                                W. S. GILBERT: *Patience*

THE phrase was invented by James Branch Cabell
for *The Richmond Reviewer*, which he secretly edited
for three months, but to the extent that payment was
never in specie it applied to most of the Little Magazines
which during the 'twenties lent to the literary scene the
esoteric note that, in a thousand remodeled barns, the
Little Theater movement was giving the stage. Few of
the Little Magazines were ever out of the red, and what
little money they took in went to printers who did not
share their employers' enthusiasm for the literary renaissance and for revolt. There wasn't much money, anyway.
Advertisements were usually sold for about twenty-five
dollars a page, and subscription lists rarely reached five
hundred copies.

Writers did not mind — very much — and they kept
the Little Magazine editors supplied with an abundance
of material from which to make up their tables of con-

tents. It is true that most of the writers were beginners, but many who could command five cents a word from commercial publications wrote gratis for the Little Magazines in convincing proof that, however business-minded writers generally are, they are sometimes capable of sacrifices upon the altar of Art.

The Little Magazine movement was not strictly a product of the 'twenties. Fugitive, belligerent little publications had sprung up by the time Germany invaded Belgium, and in 1916 Robert J. Coady founded one called *The Soil* which set a standard for impudence and novelty by deifying Chaplin, African sculpture, prize-fighting, Gertrude Stein, slang, and dressmaking as an art, and by printing an entire Nick Carter novel on the grounds that for 'straight and swift narration the dime-novel has not yet been surpassed.' But it was during the 'twenties that they reached their pinnacle in number and influence, and by the time of the stock-market crash, the Little Magazine movement as a literary force was dead.

The Little Magazine was distinguished from other publications most easily by the fact that it did not make money. It was owned by its editors, who served without salary, and frequently had to go into their own pockets to pay the printer. Sometimes there was not even a printer. *The Gyroscope*, a poetry magazine issued from Palo Alto, California, was mimeographed by its editors, Janet Lewis and Yvor Winters. But most of the Little Magazine editors would have been irritated at a definition deduced from bank balance figures. The Little Magazines, in their opinion, were a healthy, vital, necessary, and artistically important phenomenon; they were liberating the poet and the story-teller from the restrictions imposed by publications which existed by appealing to the masses; they were discovering and encouraging new literary talents; they were providing an experimental laboratory for new art forms and points of view; in brief, they were creating a new literature.

Usually they were run with a charming informality. Ideas for articles and stories developed at parties, and manuscripts were accepted or rejected after discussions lightened by highballs. Editors, free from the necessity of pleasing stockholders, did not have to consider racial, religious, or esthetic prejudices when they pondered over a manuscript. Nor did they have to think of the advertisers. Popular magazines of huge circulations have a list of taboos imposed by space-buyers; for instance, one of them will not print a story in which an automobile accident is caused by the blowing out of a tire, for the tire manufacturers would be offended. The Little Magazine editor paid no attention to this restriction, if indeed he had ever heard of it. He was free to print, within the limits of the postal laws, anything he chose.

The result was refreshing novelty in a field that had hitherto been ruled largely by the editorial stereotypes. One opened one's latest copy of a Little Magazine with the zest with which a modern tested the wares of a new bootlegger. Those who opened a certain issue of *The Little Review* found a novel called *Ulysses* which ran:

> Imperthnthn thnthnthn
> Chips, picking chips off rocky thumbnail,
> Horrid! And gold flushed more.

And one issue of *The Reviewer* carried a poem by Robert Nathan called 'Joan to her Father' which described a little girl's attitude toward sitting on her pottie.

Since it was novelty that got attention, novelty was vastly overemphasized, and if the Little Magazine had any defect greater than its instability, it was a tendency toward sensationalism. *The Folio*, published in New York, surprised readers by having each of the contributors — artists, writers, and musicians — responsible for his own page. (He also paid for publishing it.) *The Little Review* was constantly bringing out special editions — an all-American edition, a revaluation of Henry James edition, a machine-age edition, an international theater edition. No esthetic idea was too incomprehensible or too insane to get a hearing in one of the Little Magazines. No trick of style, no innovation in punctuation, spelling, or grammar was too strange to go without its champion.

POETRY FINDS A MARKET

NOT all the Little Magazines were intellectually immature, dedicated to raising the hair or cutting throats. Some of them published first-rate material. They encouraged many young writers who have since justified their promise. They got a hearing for writers who deserved a hearing, but for one reason or another had been rejected by the commercial magazines. In the field of poetry they were particularly praiseworthy, for poetry notoriously interests few readers, and the standard magazines published very little of it. Poetry magazines sprang up by the score during the decade, representing every shade of method, idea, and style.

The best of them, by all odds, was not a product of the decade, but was founded as long ago as 1912, and is flourishing today. It is *Poetry: A Magazine of Verse.* In its columns Harriet Monroe, its founder and editor, published much of the best verse of our times. Ezra Pound, Edgar Lee Masters, Robert Frost, Vachel Lindsay, H. D. (Hilda Doolittle), Carl Sandburg, Maxwell Bodenheim, and others of varying poetic philosophies appeared in her pages. In addition, she carried penetrating and enlightened discussions of poetry.

But one of the most interesting poetry magazines published during the 'twenties, *The Fugitive* of Nashville, Tennessee, was definitely of the period, even down to the smart-alecky foreword with which, in 1922, it began publication:

> Official exception having been taken by the sovereign people to the mint julep, a literary phrase known rather euphemistically as Southern Literature has expired, like any other stream whose source has stopped up. The demise was not untimely; among other advantages, *The Fugitive* is enabled to come to birth in Nashville, Tennessee, under a star not entirely unsympathetic. *The Fugitive* flees from nothing faster than from the high-caste Brahmins of the Old South. Without raising the question of whether the blood in the veins of its editors runs red, they at any rate are not advertising it as blue; indeed, as to pedigree, they cheerfully invite the most unfavorable inference from the circumstances of their anonymity.

Behind this anonymity were Allen Tate, the anti-Humanist, who has written several books of poetry and a few biographies; John Crowe Ransom, author of *Grace Before Meat, Chills and Fever*, and other volumes of verse; Donald Davidson, author of *The Tall Men*, a book of poetry; James Marshall Frank, Sidney Mitron-Hirsch, Stanley Johnson, and Alec B. Stevenson. They did not remain anonymous very long, and soon they were producing an excellent and influential magazine, attracting the older poets and many younger ones — John Donald Wade, Andrew Nelson Lytle, and Robert Penn Warren — to their banner.

Poetry: A Magazine of Verse and *The Fugitive* were the best of the verse publications of the decade, but there were a host of them that from time to time published distinguished work. In fact there were so many poetry magazines that their editors found it difficult to find appropriate names for them, and the decade saw magazines bearing titles which might have applied equally well to motor cars, canned goods, or cosmetics. *Tempo* was founded by Oliver Jenkins in Danvers, Massachusetts, in 1921, to bring out ultra-modern verse. There were *Rhythmus; The Nomad*, in Alabama, which published Carl Carmer; *The Lyric*, at Norfolk, Virginia, which brought out John Moreland, Virginia McCormick, Mary Sinton Leitch, Virginia Lyne Tunstall, Josephine Johnson, and Julia Johnson Davis; *The Circle*, published in Baltimore, where Lizette Woodworth Reese reigned as high priestess; *Pagan, Measure, Contemporary Verse, The Lyric West*, edited by Grace Atherton Dennen in Los Angeles, *Voices, Parnassus, The Lariat, Star-Dust, The Forge, The Muse, Palo Verde*, and many others.

GENESIS OF A MAGAZINE

THESE were strictly poetry magazines, but all the Little Magazines published verse, a greater percentage of it than the commercial publications. *The Reviewer* brought out Babette Deutsch, Jean Starr Untermeyer, Bodenheim, George Sterling, Vincent Starrett, Henry Bellaman, Elinor Wylie, Du Bose Heyward, John Galsworthy, and Louis Untermeyer. The genesis of this magazine was a party in Richmond at which *This Side of Paradise* and *Jurgen* were so heatedly discussed that those present decided they, too, must have a part in the exciting new literary renaissance. Margaret Freeman, who later became an interior decorator, promised to solicit enough advertising from local merchants to keep the publication going for six months, and Mary Dallas Street put up two hundred dollars to print and mail a prospectus. Emily Clark, author of a scandalous book of sketches called *Stuffed Peacocks*, undertook the thankless task of soliciting gratis contributions; Hunter Stagg took over the reviewing end.

The first issue, appearing in February, 1921, had a great piece of good fortune. Mencken's *Prejudices: Second Series* was just out and Stagg reviewed it. This volume contained Mencken's celebrated denunciation of the South, 'The Sahara of the Bozart.' The essay was calculated to enrage the average Southerner, but Stagg took it calmly enough. He praised the book, and admitted that many of the charges against the South were true. Surprised and delighted, Mencken, to whom a copy had been sent, wrote to the editors to offer his powerful assistance. Soon he was appearing in the magazine, and helping it to get contributors. Others assisted in this enterprise, including Cabell, Van Vechten, Hergesheimer, and Alfred A. Knopf, and on occasion *The Reviewer* had the most distinguished list of contributors on the magazine stands.

Besides the poets, there were Ellen Glasgow, Hergesheimer, Mary Johnston, Agnes Repplier, Ben Ray Redman, Burton Rascoe, Henrie Waste, Edwin Björkman, Ernest Boyd, Frances Newman, Julia Peterkin, Douglas Goldring, Arthur Machen, Ronald Firbank, Edwin Muir, and Edward Hale Bierstadt — these in addition to a score of young writers who appeared first in its pages and have since been paid money for their writings.

But in spite of an impressive table of contents, a high standard of writing, and good notices in the papers, *The Reviewer* had hard sledding during its entire career. It ran for six months as a bi-weekly, then shut down. Again Miss Street put up the necessary cash, and after an interim of two months it was resumed as a monthly. Nine months later it was suspended again, but was reborn as a quarterly, with a descendant of Thomas White, who had hired Edgar Allan Poe as editor of *The Southern Literary Messenger*, as business manager. When a mounting pile of bills threatened extinction, the Poe Shrine in Richmond offered the magazine a part of its building and some financial assistance. This offer was accepted, but the dissatisfied editors decided after two months that they would rather suspend than continue under this aegis.

Just then a Northern friend of the magazine put up some cash, and it continued on its own for another year. In December, 1924, Paul Green came up from the University of North Carolina with an offer to take it over. He moved it to Chapel Hill, where, though he paid his contributors a cent a word, he was unable to keep up its old quality: perhaps writers preferred donating outright to working for so little. After a year, Green turned his interests toward the Carolina Playmakers and the dramas which were to bring him fame and fortune, and *The Reviewer* became, in Don Marquis's description of an Egyptian mummy, quite deceased.

The Reviewer made its debut at about the time *The Double Dealer* was bowing before the New Orleans *literati*. *The Double Dealer* was started by young people just out of college. Its guiding genius was John McClure, who succeeded in editing the magazine, writing a deal of quite good verse, and holding a job on the copy desk of the *Times-Picayune* at the same time. *The Double Dealer* exhumed from New Orleans newspapers forgotten essays by Lafcadio Hearn, published articles attempting to show that the South was the most productive section of the country in a literary way, and otherwise was less cosmopolitan than *The Reviewer*. Lacking *The Reviewer* editors' talent for getting highly paid writers to contribute for nothing, McClure was never able to attract the attentions that were showered upon his contemporary. But he brought out a creditable magazine every month, and he too introduced to the world a number of writers who have since become more or less famous.

HECHT AND HIS TIMES

THESE two Southern magazines were fairly orthodox in their editorial policies, though *The Reviewer* printed the inanities of Gertrude Stein, but most of the Little Magazines were more startling. *S_4N*, published in Northampton, Massachusetts, by Norman Fitts, believed in 'the principle of growth through disagreement,' and exemplified this principle by printing Thornton Wilder, Gorham B. Munson, Hart Crane, and William Lyon Phelps, thus contriving to annoy at least half its readers all the time. *The Guardian* attempted to prove that Philadelphia need no longer be 'suburban to Cosmopolis.'

Of all the Little Magazines, the most sensational was the *Chicago Literary Times*, which took unorthodoxy to the extreme of appearing in the format of a tabloid newspaper. The *Times*, produced by Ben Hecht and the other 'self-made men of letters' of the Middle West, was impudent, scandalous, highly journalistic. It even used newspaper headlines and 'leads,' a typical caption being: 'Bodenheim runs amuck; six killed, five injured.' Under this headline Bodenheim ran devastating epigrammatic remarks on eleven writers of whom he disapproved. The *Times* went in strongly for epigrams. Hecht called Hugh Walpole 'an amiable mediocrity,' Sir Oliver Lodge 'a befuddled old man capitalizing his dotage,' and Carl Sandburg 'an untrained prestidigitator surprised at the

rabbits he pulls out of a plug hat.' When Joseph Conrad
on his American trip was receiving the adulation of critics,
interviewers, and editorial writers everywhere else, Hecht
disposed of him by calling him a 'writer for grocery-
men.'

Hecht was the leader of the Chicago literary school,
which for a few years was the most exciting group of
writing men in the country. He seemed to be able to do
anything. Several of his news stories, one of them a
description of a hanging, and his sketches called *A Thousand and One Afternoons in Chicago*, are by way of being
journalistic classics. His novel *Erik Dorn* was a brilliant
tour de force in irony, wit, and disillusionment. He turned
to the stage with great popular success, and when Hollywood lured him he proved he could put more box-office
appeal into a scenario than anybody else on the lots.

Hecht has now given himself up altogether to the pursuit of popularity and riches, and it is doubtful if he will
ever again produce much of literary dignity. He seems
destined to be a literary lost hope like Robert W. Chambers and Rupert Hughes, though he is never as insipid or
as obvious as Chambers and Hughes got to be at the
height of their money-making powers.

A crony of Hecht's in conceiving the *Chicago Literary
Times* — and also a Chicago *Daily News* alumnus — was
Carl Sandburg, who wrote unorthodox poetry about
trains, stockyards, and other unpoetical subjects. Sandburg expressed his own creed more effectively than the
critics will ever be able to put it: 'I am credulous,' he
wrote, 'about the destiny of man, the future of the race,
and the importance of illusions. I should like to be in the

same moment an earthworm (which I am) and a rider to the moon (which I am).'

Sandburg paradoxically combined an interest in the facts of manufacture and transportation with a passion for ballads and old songs, which he went around the country with a banjo collecting. Once a distinguished Frenchman came to see him. They knew little about each other, and for a long while there was an embarrassing silence. To make conversation, Sandburg gave his visitor such information as the amount of coal mined in Illinois, and the number of miles from Chicago to Dallas. Puzzled, the Frenchman was about to go when Sandburg began singing sentimental ballads and Negro songs. The Frenchman later said it was the most delightful evening he had spent in America. He came back for another session, and while the two were engrossed in old songs, a thief entered the house and stole the Frenchman's luggage and money.

Reminiscent of Whitman in many ways, Sandburg sang of America with a chip on the shoulder. Why, he asked, did not Americans perceive that names like Omaha, Medicine Hat, and Kenosha were as lovely as Milano, Venezia, and Padova? He wrote in an idiom so 'American' that at first only the Little Magazines would publish his poems. This is typical Sandburg:

> All I can give you is broken face gargoyles,
> It is too early to sing and dance at funerals.
> Though I can whisper to you I am looking for an undertaker
>   humming a lullaby and throwing his feet in a swift and
>   mystic buck-and-wing, and now you see it and now you
>   don't.

STAR OF THE CHICAGO GROUP

MORE important than Hecht or Sandburg, though lacking the dramatic talents of the former and the poetical gifts of the latter, was Sherwood Anderson, another member of the Chicago group and one of the strangest figures of the decade. Anderson, a native of Ohio, had little formal schooling, wandering from town to town with his father, whom he described as 'a lovable, improvident fellow, inclined to stretch the truth in statement... colorful, no-account, who should have been a novelist himself.'

He was forced to go to work for a living at the age of twelve, holding all sorts of odd jobs. He served in the Spanish-American War, and returning found himself something of a local hero. He got a job as manager of a factory, but the work was too dull for him, and in the middle of a letter he was dictating to his stenographer, he decided to give up business. Leaving his stenographer certain he was insane, he put on his hat and walked out of town. His brother Karl was a magazine illustrator in Chicago, and there he went, getting a job as an advertising copy writer. He was successful in advertising, though he missed the distinction of William Rose Benét, who created the slogan, 'The petal texture of a baby's skin,' for Mennen's Talcum Powder and 'Your house under glass' for Murphy's Varnish, but this job did not appeal to him any more than running a paint factory.

Meanwhile, stimulated by Hecht, Floyd Dell, Llewellyn Jones, and other members of the Chicago group, he began writing stories — strange, half-articulate stories of the secret, shabby dreams of lonely and beaten men. A typical Anderson theme is that of his story 'The Triumph of the Egg,' which was also the title of the volume of short stories which won him the Dial Prize in 1921. The central character of the story is a man who runs a little all-night eating-place in a 'hello town.' He sees the drummers come in, men with an air of the great world and a repertory of fascinating stories. He envies them. He, too, wants to shine before his fellows, to project his personality, to become a person rather than just the man behind the lunch counter. Finally, in a frenzy of frustration, he tells a group of customers he can perform an extraordinary trick with eggs. He says this on an impulse which he cannot understand, for he has never tried the trick in his life. Interested, the customers gather around. He undertakes the feat, fails. The egg is crushed in his hand. The customers leave, laughing at his ineptitude and humiliation.

Told baldly, this seems a mere low-comedy episode. As Anderson handled it, the story becomes extraordinarily moving, profound, and pathetic. This groping for secrets of the heart and mind that other writers have not concerned themselves with is characteristic of Anderson. At times he succeeds brilliantly, but at other times his themes are too elusive, too deeply buried in the subconscious, for his talents.

Edward J. O'Brien, a distinguished poet who turned short story anthologist, gave Anderson and Ernest Hem-

REST AFTER REVOLT
Sherwood Anderson bought two weeklies, and settled in the Virginia hills

ingway much of the credit for the improvement in the American short story which marked the decade. Under their stimulus and that of Whit Burnett and Martha Foley with their *Story Magazine*, short-story writers began to exhibit the qualities of freshness of observation and boldness of imagination which distinguished the better novelists.

The Little Magazines were at first Anderson's only market. Jane Heap and Margaret Anderson published him in *The Little Review*; later *The Dial* and Mencken took him up. He made little money, but that did not bother him. When *Windy McPherson's Son* finally appeared (Anderson was offered publication immediately after he wrote it if he would make certain revisions, but he refused to change a line), one of the popular magazines saw in it qualities which indicated Anderson could write commercially successful fiction. A representative was sent to see him. He explained to Anderson how the novel could have been revised to make it a popular serial. The revision he suggested would have stripped the novel of its merits as a work of art. Anderson listened politely. At the end of the exposition, he told the magazine representative to go to hell, and showed him the door.

Years later Anderson made some money — with *Dark Laughter* — but he has always written what and when the 'obscure inner necessity' of Conrad moved him to write. The money from *Dark Laughter* made it possible for him to buy a beautiful home and two weekly newspapers in Marion, Virginia, a town of a few thousand persons, and there he settled, he thought permanently, after a period of restless roaming to Paris, New Orleans, and other cities. When news got about that Anderson was going to live in Marion, a mountaineer preacher warned his flock from the pulpit that an atheist and a believer in free love was coming among them. Anderson was hospitably received, however; the people were proud to have in their midst a man who had written books and whose picture had been in the papers. Admirers elsewhere — in New York, Paris, and London — subscribed to his papers in such numbers that his postage bill forced him to discontinue out-of-state circulation.

Anderson had hilarious adventures in country journalism. When he took over the papers — one Democratic and one Republican, in a county that was almost evenly divided politically — he found no one had ever run a full-page advertisement in them. Anderson finally induced a local merchant to take a page. Later the merchant came in to complain that he had been charged for the page at a rate higher than was charged for smaller advertisement. 'I'm not very good at figures,' Anderson later told a friend, 'and when I multiplied the number of inches in a page by the amount per inch, I got the wrong answer. I had to think fast. Luckily, I got an idea. "Look here," I said, "you have to pay something for dominating this paper." I got away with it.'

In the quiet mountain country, running his papers as he chose, driving alone over the cool, smooth roads every night, Anderson at last found peace and contentment. He was convinced he would stay there the rest of his life, and he became convinced, too, that country journalism is the ideal field for the somewhat literary young person who objects to the harsh restrictions of daily newspapering: he even went on a lecture tour to expound this idea to college boys and girls. But after a few years the old restlessness seized him again, and he turned the papers over to his son so he could wander when he pleased.

THE LIVELY MERCURY

IF ANDERSON never appeared in the popular magazines, he was a favored contributor to *The American Mercury*, which reached the highest circulation of the so-called quality group. He was in the second issue with a short story called 'Caught,' and was heavily advertised in Volume One, Number One, which appeared in January, 1924, and instantly sold out as news of Ernest Boyd's debunking 'Esthete: Model 1924' got about.

The Mercury, 'a green-backed mark of intellectual distinction,' was a descendant of *The Smart Set*, which Mencken and Nathan had been running for some years. In its pages Mencken continued to do the books, and George Jean Nathan, an Indianaian who owned thirty-eight overcoats, three dinner suits, and fourteen walking sticks, continued a theater column in which he worshiped Eugene O'Neill and sneered at almost everybody else. '*Répétition Générale*' in the old *Smart Set* — a department of pert comments on life and letters — went over into *The Mercury* as 'Clinical Notes.'

Smart Set had dealt almost exclusively in fiction, poetry, and epigrams. The magazine appealed to the enthusiastic young and the spuriously 'arty' who considered politics, economics, and allied subjects beneath their notice. When Mencken on one occasion printed an eulogy of Senator James Reed of Missouri he apologized to 'the intelligentsia' for obtruding politics upon their notice. *The Mercury*, however, went in heavily for politics and the social and natural sciences, carrying little fiction, less poetry, and no epigrams at all. Its first issue contained an essay on Abraham Lincoln's paternity, and articles on disarmament, Senator Hiram Johnson of California, communism, architecture, glands, war, New Thought, police methods, and George Santayana. There were only two short stories, and Theodore Dreiser contributed the only poetry.

The Mercury's influence was perhaps unparalleled in American magazine history. Endeavoring to appeal to what its editors called 'the civilized minority,' it was skeptical, ironical, polished, and learned. The Young Intellectuals adopted it as their organ, for it led the fight against the academicians and the reformers, and it published the work of the writers who were most admired by the young — Cabell, Fitzgerald, Hergesheimer, Boyd, and the others. Collegians carried the magazine to classes to annoy their professors, and fledgling intellectuals were described by each other as readers of *The Mercury*. So widely was held the belief that readers of the magazine were cultured and otherwise 'superior' persons that this classified advertisement appeared in the *Peninsula Daily Herald* of Monterey, California: 'Wanted — Young widow would like position as housekeeper for

single gentleman of simple tastes. Subscriber to *American
Mercury* preferred.'

The announcement of policy published in the first issue
of the magazine (which, incidentally, later sold for as
high as fifty dollars a copy) was a gem of self-advertising:

> The Editors have heard no Voice from the burning bush.
> They will not cry up and offer for sale any sovereign balm,
> whether political, economic, or esthetic, for all the sorrows
> of the world. The fact is, indeed, that they doubt that
> any such sovereign balm exists, or that it will ever exist
> hereafter. The world, as they see it, is down with at least
> a score of painful diseases, all of them chronic and in-
> curable; nevertheless, they cling to the notion that human
> existence remains predominantly charming. Especially
> it is charming in this unparalleled Republic of the West,
> where men are earnest and women are intelligent, and all
> the historic virtues of Christendom are now concentrated.
> The Editors propose, before jurisprudence develops to the
> point of prohibiting skepticism altogether, to give a realistic
> consideration to certain of these virtues, and to try to save
> what is exhilarating in them, even when all that is divine
> must be abandoned. They engage to undertake the busi-
> ness in a polished and aseptic manner, without indignation
> on the one hand and without much regard for tender feel-
> ings on the other. They have no set program, either de-
> structive or constructive. Sufficient unto each day will
> be the performance thereof.

In general it lived up to this credo, debunking during
the decade almost every stuffed shirt and every fallacy
widely held in America, whether political, medical, artistic,
historical, or scientific. Mencken has high talents as an
editor (Nathan, who was interested only in 'the surface,
the color of life,' withdrew from the partnership, and
Mencken carried on alone), and he contrived to get together a lively list of topics for each issue.

Perhaps the most popular feature of the magazine, however, was not the aseptic and polished consideration of ideas held by the 'booboosie,' as Mencken called the masses, but a symposium headed 'Americana' in which they exposed their own idiocies. 'Americana,' devoted to clippings of the pathetic and idiotic doings of Americans, was sometimes hilariously funny, but it had its value for students, too. It ran clippings like these, a score or more to an issue. From a speech by W. A. MacRae, former commissioner of agriculture in Florida: 'Development of real estate in Florida had its historic precedent many thousand years before Christ. In fact, it is mentioned in the Book of Genesis, being one of the first acts recorded in Holy Writ.' From the Sioux City, Nebraska, *Journal*: 'The house of representatives by a rising vote congratulated Wayne [Big] Munn for taking the world's heavyweight championship from Strangler Lewis.' From a speech by Edward Scheve to the Huntington Park (California) Club: 'Tolstoi was an unconscious Kiwanian.'

As the decade drew to a close, the first high enthusiasm for *The Mercury* began to subside. The magazine was no longer quoted as frequently as it had been in its youth, and circulation began to decline. Mencken tried several devices to keep it going — an editorial in the front, a series of 'reports' on civilization in various states, a department devoted to music, an amusing attempt to determine by statistics which was the 'worst American state' (it turned out to be Mississippi) — but it continued to slip.

Perhaps Mencken, after all, was the chief asset of the magazine, and in time he began to repeat himself; two of his major crusades had succeeded when the back of censorship was broken and the majority of the people fell in line with his view of the Eighteenth Amendment. A more plausible explanation is that readers tired of the efforts of other contributors to imitate Mencken's style. It was easy to reproduce Mencken's surface manner — his use of foreign phrases, his antitheses, his employment of the double negative in short powerful sentences — but in other hands they seemed forced and artificial. Save for the comparatively few well-known writers with individual styles — Cabell, Hergesheimer, Anderson and Company — all his contributors wrote like so many parrots.

Worse, they handled their subjects according to formula, and when the reader began an article by an unknown journalist, he knew in advance not only how it was going to be written but how the fallacy under examination was to be exploded. If young contributors did not adhere to the formula, they were told to, and surprised writers found, upon receiving proofs of their articles, that they had been pointed up to be more devastating than intended. (When they objected they were permitted to say exactly what they wanted to say.) And this began to weary the readers. There is often a vicious circle in magazine publishing. The editor hits upon a successful formula, and since it is successful he does not alter it. In time the formula itself becomes tiresome, and often this is not realized until it is too late to adopt another policy.

GENTLE TOLERANCE

OF THE 'Quality' magazines of the decade, the two most widely read by the New Generation were *The Mercury* and *The Bookman*. They had little in common. *The Mercury* was in the nature of a monthly blast, and its point of view was always precisely the same. The contents of *The Bookman* were largely information, and it presented all points of view with a tolerance which *The Mercury* boasted it possessed but rarely exhibited. Like *Poetry: A Magazine of Verse*, *The Bookman* was not a product of the decade. In fact, it was started in February, 1895, publishing in its first issue Sir James Barrie's 'Scotland's Lament.' When the 'twenties began it had, under the editorship of Robert Cortes Holliday, an elderly, kind, editor's-easy-chair aspect. It was pretty dull. It contained routine information about books and writers — what was being published, what was selling, where writers were living, and what they ate — but the information was presented in *World Almanac* style. Book reviews generally were written with a bored, lifeless air, and a fair sample of the verse was a poem called 'Comparison,' by Ruth Lambert Jones, published in the issue of September, 1919:

> You say: 'How tiring it must be
> To weave ballads constantly!'
>
> I cry: 'What weariness must sway
> One who plants gardens all the day!'

Yet I don't tire of making songs
Nor does your sowing weary you,
Because each to his task belongs
And does what he loves well to do.

The magazine took on life early in the decade when John Farrar became editor. Farrar was a poet, a playwright, a literary critic, a dramatic critic, and an industrious editor. He quickly corralled for *The Bookman* all the young reviewers who were beginning to make a splash in the world — Heywood Broun, Robert Benchley, Sidney Howard, Laurence Stallings, Hershell Brickell, and others. The magazine carried from time to time a score of features — anonymous 'spotlights' of contemporary writers, Donald Ogden Stewart's and Corey Ford's parodies, statements of philosophy by various writers, debates on such subjects as book clubs, movie reviews, modern criticism of novels that have become classics, and 'lessons' for women's clubs. In addition were carried gossip of writers, notes on the literary life of foreign countries, best-seller lists, and notices, if not reviews, of practically all books of general interest published in America.

In spite of its variety and appeal to different literary groups, the magazine did not make money, and when George H. Doran sold it in the fall of 1927, it was announced that it had been operated at a loss for nine years. The magazine was always subject to criticism because Doran was also a book publisher, though a careful examination of its files shows that Doran books were never unduly publicized and that the productions of rival publishers were treated with fairness and hospitality. The magazine was sold to Burton Rascoe and Seward Collins, but soon

Rascoe withdrew and Collins converted it into a Humanist organ, publishing T. S. Eliot, Norman Foerster, Hamlin Garland, and Irving Babbitt, denouncing Mencken, and lamenting the alleged apostasy of Stuart P. Sherman. Later *The Bookman* disappeared as a magazine title, and the Bookman Publishing Company, owned by Collins, published a thin gray quarterly called *The American Review* which was the spokesman for the Agrarian movement in the South and the Distributists of England.

'QUALITY' AND POPULAR MAGAZINES

THE other 'Quality Group' magazines — *Scribner's, Harpers, Century, The Atlantic Monthly* — in time reflected the spirit of the New Generation. As the circulation of *The Mercury* soared and it lent ever fresh luster to the book-publishing house of Alfred A. Knopf, rival magazines quietly 'modernized' their editorial policies. *Harpers* did not go modern until September of 1925, but *Scribner's* before then had recognized the existence of the younger generation, and the consequent demand for greater frankness and liveliness. *Scribner's* brought out Ernest Hemingway, F. Scott Fitzgerald, and Ring Lardner before Lardner became a pet of the intellectuals. *Century* printed Anderson and Ruth Suckow and T. S. Stribling's *Birthright* serially, though in spite of this and spectacular experiments in format, it fought a losing battle against dwindling circulation.

To some extent the editors of all the popular magazines of huge circulations followed the example of *Harper's Bazaar*, which in 1921 decided to run serials by the younger writers. *Harper's Bazaar* inaugurated the policy with Stephen Vincent Benét's novel *Young People's Pride*. Even the *Saturday Evening Post*, more conservative than *Cosmopolitan*, *Collier's*, or any of its other competitors, engaged the author of *This Side of Paradise* for frequent contributions. *The Post*, with its more than two million circulation, remained extremely conservative — its fiction did not admit that women smoked and it rejected large quantities of advertising which it considered questionable but which almost any other publication in the country would have accepted gladly.

Perhaps because of its policies it was fashionable among the younger 'arty' people in the twenties to denounce the *Post* as bourgeois and stupid (George Horace Lorimer, its editor, said, 'The editor of a popular magazine is unpopular with all critics except those who contribute or who hope to contribute to his magazine'); but actually it published a high percentage of first-rate material. It brought out Dreiser, Fitzgerald, and Hergesheimer, among others; it was the first magazine — this was long before the decade opened — to serialize a novel by James Branch Cabell. It has always been hospitable to young writers and novel ideas, and it had the very fine virtue of paying its writers enough to live on decently.

College Humor was an interesting magazine which came in with the younger generation and began slipping when they grew older. Founded by H. N. Swanson, a young man of enormous enthusiasm and high editorial talent, it offered entertainment to the more intelligent tea-dancers at the Plaza and the young men and women on a thousand campuses who would have tea-danced at the Plaza if they could have afforded to. One of Swanson's discoveries was Katharine Brush, who was later, with a slick novel called *Young Man of Manhattan*, to lift the circulation of the *Saturday Evening Post*, in which it was published serially. Another was James Aswell, who had, however, published an excellent volume of verse, *We Know Better*, before he appeared in Swanson's pages. Conforming on the surface to the slick-paper methods of lesser writers, Aswell lifted his short stories above the popular magazine standard through a fresh, individual style and a shrewd understanding of character.

After the decline of *College Humor*, Swanson went to Hollywood, where he became first a film director and later a literary agent. As an editor he followed hundreds of writers to the literary promised land. During the opulent decade Hollywood not only bought the film rights to literary productions — sometimes paying as high as twenty-five thousand dollars for a novel — but imported writers to compose scenarios based on their own and others' work and to give technical advice on the translation of plots from wood pulp to celluloid. Hollywood, always prodigal with money and dominated by the philosophy that costliness is the criterion of merit, paid some of its writers three thousand dollars a week, on which they could, and did, mix with the Fairbankses and the Talmadges on terms of artistic and social equality. All too often Hollywood forgot about its writers after it bought them, leaving them with no duties other than drawing their salary checks. In one case a film company forgot to remove a playwright's name from the payroll when his contract had expired. He drew his check for five weeks before the error was discovered.

It is a commonplace of criticism to blame Hollywood for the failure of talented writers, like Rupert Hughes, to achieve their early promise. Like many platitudes, the percentage of error here is high. The novelist or short story writer who is ambitious to sell to the movies need not concoct movie plots for his publishers, for the simple reason that Hollywood changes the plots of the stories it buys to suit its purpose. From time to time during the decade a writer rose in artistic wrath to denounce the movies for garbling his story and his meaning. The complaint was naïve and childish. A writer who does not realize when he signs the contract that his work is likely to be altered has necessarily been living away from all contact with the printed word and places where movies may be seen.

The movies did provide the chute to literary oblivion, however, for several promising writers who went to Hollywood to work directly for the films. Becoming grooved to the demands of the film magnates for stories appealing to millions of people, they found it difficult to write for the few when they tried. Ben Hecht was an example; a highly successful movie scenario writer, his literary work degenerated from the brilliance of his early books to the point where it became almost unreadable. In this and other cases, however, the movies only provided the sliding board; the primary defect was in the artist.

The magazine of the decade which most clearly expressed the editorial yearnings of the New Generation managed to survive the New Generation and, having subtly shifted its emphasis as tastes and prejudices changed, is a commercial success now. *The New Yorker* was started in February of 1925, by Harold Ross with an idea which he understood quite clearly, but which always was a little nebulous to the procession of his managing editors, which his friends called 'the Jesus parade.' Ross found it difficult to explain to his associates precisely what he wanted, but by endless experimentation and trial and error he finally produced *The New Yorker* formula.

This formula, an expression of the decade, is to take nothing seriously — politics, economic theories, social reform, or art. It wars on pretentiousness, but not with the indignation of *The Mercury*; it is gentle, ironic, and at all times and above everything it attempts to be witty. It exhibits great variety — from the half-mad drawings of James Thurber to the conventional journalism of Morris Markey, but always as though to say, 'This is sophisticated stuff, and if you understand and like it, you are a sophisticated person.' Originally smart-alecky and contemptuous of anything not by, for, and of New York, the magazine gradually became more tolerant, less complacent, and as it matured it ceased to be a fad and became what appears to be a permanent member of the magazine company.

The magazines of the 'twenties, then, reflected the emergence, revolt, and growing up of the post-war generation as accurately as the books that were published. At least one of them was devoted to every new esthetic, political, and social theory propounded. They were the fast-moving cavalry of the revolt against staidness and conservatism. And if the younger generation did not capture all the magazines, neither did it capture all the book sales. There were *The Little Review* and Dadaism, but likewise there were *Good Housekeeping* and Harold Bell Wright.

VIII. RAISING EYEBROWS

VIII. RAISING EYEBROWS

'I have no f-f-f-friends,' retorted the Duke. 'Only people
that amuse me, and people I sleep with.'

CARL VAN VECHTEN: *The Blind Bow-Boy*

SHOCKING readers 'would, after all, be a rather hard
thing to do in these outspoken days,' wrote a reviewer
in 1919, and the following year Charles Hanson Towne
remarked, with the superiority of one safely a part of a
polite literary world, that 'the sex story has had its exultant hour.... Like the dancing craze, it preceded the war.'

It became immediately apparent that these statements
were quite wrong (Towne's faith in himself as a prophet no
doubt quailed further before the onslaught of the Black
Bottom and the Charleston). Authors were to prove con-
clusively that it was an easy matter to shock readers in
these outspoken days and that, far from being a dead
issue, the sex story could rise to far more exultant heights
than it had before the war. They were to proclaim that
homosexuality, incest, prostitution (male and female),
miscegenation, impotence, venereal disease, abortion, and
masturbation were fit subjects for artistic treatment, and
they were to follow up their proclamation with concrete
examples. A character in Van Vechten's *The Blind Bow-
Boy* was to inquire: 'Have you heard about Bunny? He's
had Zimbule's name tattooed on his person so cunningly
that it can only be deciphered under certain conditions';
and Sadie Thompson on the stage of *Rain* was to fire in the

face of a missionary, 'You goddamn, psalm-singing son-of-a-bitch!'

Dismayed and shocked Elders thought of the peaceful days when the 1893 edition of Fielding's *Joseph Andrews* rendered the word 'zounds' as 'z——s' and Parson Adams, in explaining marriage rules to Joseph said, 'As many as are joined together otherwise than G——'s word doth allow are not joined together by G——.' But post-war writers were not to mention 'G——' at all except in lusty goddamn-dialogue; they preferred instead 'dirty punks, heels, bastards,' as did the authors of *The Front Page*.

What caused it? What flooded the river of bawdiness that churned through the literature of the 'twenties? *The Saturday Review of Literature* answered: 'It is a war neurosis; it is relief from undue suppressions; in part it is a response to an obscure psychologic change which has shaken youth free from age and negated the sanctions of tradition and experience; in part it is the decay of formal religion and its controls.' In short, the mirror that writers were holding up to life was reflecting accurately, and fiction was following its traditional job with more than traditional conscientiousness. The lid of decorum had exploded from the cauldron of well-mannered reticence and the young people were pouring out jubilantly; writers turned reporters and snared the high excitement while it lasted.

They had a fairly logical defense for their oversexed fiction, and were as raucous in using it as were their opponents in expressing hearty disapproval. It was necessary to discuss sex to give a full, well-rounded picture of character, they said. Everything written before the New Free-

dom had been lopsided: There had been no hint of the
actualities which precipitated events. A novel which was
reticent about the sexual lives of its characters was a poor
novel because it falsified moving forces. Even the conservative *Saturday Review of Literature* chimed in with 'To
restrict frankness in fiction is to stifle the imagination of a
period which science has made willing to face facts.'

Determined fact-facing certainly improved literature,
as well as making life several hundred per cent more fun.
No one in his senses hopes for a return of the James Lane
Allen type of novel, sugary and sham, as likewise no one
cares to reinstate a social system under which an adulterous woman receives a large 'A.' But, equally as certainly,
the frankness of the period was frequently perverted into
box-office uses. The youngsters protested that their battle
for freedom of sexy speech was waged for the sake of art,
but as it became increasingly apparent that naughtiness
paid — paid nice large sums — more thrills than necessary
for the presentation of 'well-rounded' character were
dished out to the agog reading public.

THE SHOCK BRIGADE

THE most fantastic example was Van Vechten's *The
Blind Bow-Boy*. Outspoken in 1923, it now reads like
a take-off of all the frank and advanced novels of the era.
It dealt with Campaspe, who 'does not know the vices,

she invents them,' and a Duke upon whose stationery was engraved, 'A thing of beauty is a boy forever,' and who eventually makes off with the likely young hero. Campaspe's son asks her what to do about an amorous roommate at school. She counters with the curiously detached question, 'Do you want to?' 'No, mama.' 'Then you don't have to.' Campaspe is smart and modern, so modern that her concession to dine with her husband is received by him as a gracious favor. (For the duration of the book she never does consent to sleep with him, probably on the ground that this is old-fashioned.) All Van Vechten's crackling, amusing dialogue (with quotation marks eliminated) and his smooth, light writing do not compensate for this heavy straining to be ultra-modern. It was wonderful sales material in the 'twenties — an advertisement of his *Firecrackers* billed him as a sort of yardstick of sophistication with 'You may test yourself by a book of Carl Van Vechten's. The degree to which you are civilized, the sharpness of your wit, and the keenness of your perceptions ——' But it did not produce fine or lasting literature in the case of *The Blind Bow-Boy*.

Floyd Dell's *The Briary Bush* took great leaps in sales when news was bruited about that it described a nude snow bath. In 1921 the dinner conversation aroused by this snow bath was almost as excited as that kindled by a later book in which an erudite whore reels off a technical list of perversions in her efforts to interest a customer. When in *Cytherea* Hergesheimer had Savina cry to a man almost a stranger, 'I want to be outraged!' matrons who felt the same yearnings hurried to buy one of the sexiest books of the decade. *Cytherea*, although an excellent analysis of sex restlessness, is sprinkled with dialogue of the same type Dorothy Speare used so lavishly. A movie actress, who otherwise closely resembles Hergesheimer's admiring 'April-moon' conception of Lillian Gish, says, 'We are not made of sugar and spice and other pleasant bits, but only of two: prostitute and mother.' Lovely young Claire announces she'd 'a damn sight rather spin a roulette wheel than rock a cradle,' a paraphrase of Dorothy Speare's 'You know you're as bored as I am ... but everyone's afraid to say what they really think about married life.'

Miss Speare was an expert at camouflaging provocative situations from the censors. For instance, 'The evening was a frost so far; 10.30 and she'd only kissed three men' was given as an illustration of the depravity of the younger generation. The book told of debutantes' drawing caricatures on bare knees, all-night petting parties, drunken girls, and amorous men, but through it all ran the current of Miss Speare's stern disapproval.

Other authors baited the censors with naughty titles. Products came out with such tags as Viña Delmar's *Kept Women, Bad Girl, Loose Ladies*, and Frances Newman's *The Hard-Boiled Virgin* (a sleek narrative containing not one word of dialogue), which started the vogue for innumerable 'virgin' titles. There was Julia Peterkin's *Scarlet Sister Mary*, Warner Fabian's *Flaming Youth*, and even Rex Beach named one of his pure and he-man tales *The Mating Call*. Maxwell Bodenheim's *Replenishing Jessica* probably sets the record; the sexual connotations of this title, however, are fulfilled in the book.

Ben Hecht was one of the chief thorns to those who considered delicacy a necessary literary trait. They stormed against *Fantazias Mallare* and *Count Bruga*, which opens with the Count taking aphrodisiacs, against *The Front Page*, on which Hecht collaborated with Charles MacArthur, when police court reporters hurled gutter epithets across the footlights, and against the scene in *Erik Dorn* when envy of a gay Lothario makes a jury acquit the woman who killed him. On the score of his bawdiness Hecht was one of the most frequently damned writers of the period. *Gargoyles* was called 'an adventure in vulgarity'; Mary Austin refers to Hecht's 'turgid, tormenting bounderism,' and Doctor Canby classifies his novels as 'phallic.'

Fitzgerald's books of the 'twenties shunned blatant sex; it was not until 1934 with the publication of *Tender is the Night* that he became 'modern' enough to treat incest. Most of his shocks were worked in through the medium of conversation and treated with the revolt in manners of the young people. 'When a man's in love with me he doesn't care for other amusements,' says one of his nineteen-year-old heroines, and 'The only thing I enjoyed was shocking people.' When her uncle speaks to her she cries: 'Will you stop boring me! Will you go 'way! Will you jump overboard and drown!' and further pleased young people who were treating their elders with the same disrespect by catching Uncle in the neck with a thrown lemon. When the husband of the gorgeous Gloria in *The Beautiful and Damned* addresses her as his wife she insists that he call her his 'permanent mistress.' Dazzling little Marjorie Harvey, a prom-trotter *de luxe*, considered that 'girls like you (her well-behaved and dull cousin) are responsible for

all the tiresome colorless marriages; all those ghastly in-
efficiencies that pass as feminine qualities. What a blow
it must be when a man with imagination marries the
beautiful bundle of clothes that he's been building ideals
round, and finds that she's just a weak, whining, cowardly
mass of affectations!... The womanly woman! Her whole
early life is occupied in whining criticisms of girls like me
who really do have a good time.'

Sinclair Lewis was reactionary enough to soft-pedal sex
in his books. Mary Austin observed of *Main Street*, 'One
wonders if he was fully aware of how much of Carol
Kennicott's failure to find herself in Gopher Prairie was
owing to the lack of sex potency, a lack which he records
without relating it to any other of her insufficiencies.'
Other successful and competent writers exhibited the
same disregard for the shocking aspects of sex. Willa
Cather, Ellen Glasgow, Edna Ferber, Edith Wharton,
Dorothy Canfield, Thornton Wilder, Thomas Beer, Booth
Tarkington, Christopher Morley, Glenway Wescott, Louis
Bromfield in their writings were quite off-hand about
physiological processes, and their characters did not use
gutter terms for these and related things. This did not
damage their box-office value; they were all habitués of
best-seller lists and reaped the just profits of the well-bred.

JURGEN AS A SEDUCER

CABELL, however, was not afflicted with such modesty, and *Jurgen*, the most discussed book of the 'twenties, shocked most readers. The scene that sent people who hadn't read a book in years scurrying to libraries (in the William and Mary College library readers were watched by guards after the theft of several copies) occurred in the chapter 'As to a Veil They Broke.' If the intervening camouflage is removed, this presentation of the seduction of a virgin stands out as a fairly lascivious bit of prose. It was art, as was pointed out by those who fought the censorship of the book, but it was lascivious none the less.

It might be noted that this scene is not an integral portion of the book; in no way is it necessary to the elaboration of Cabell's theme. It has nothing in common with the light bawdiness that features *Jurgen's* other bits of what the censors call smut — his passages on satyrs at play with oreads in the bushes, Jurgen's observance of certain strange customs of the countries he visits, his encounters with radiant women whose husbands don't understand them. It bears none of the sudden laughter of that section in *Straws and Prayer-Books*: 'I consider the new five-dollar bill which I chance this morning to possess. In itself . . . it is worth nothing: and its glazed surface chills the thought of devoting it to the one use suggested by its general dimensions.'

Hemingway in *The Sun Also Rises* picked an intrinsi-
cally more startling idea than the loss of a virginity, but
his matter-of-fact treatment reduces the reader-shock
about fifty per cent. That is, it did for those who realized
what he was talking about; it is said a portion of the public
did not grasp the pivot of the plot, that the leading male
character was incapacitated for love by a wartime wound.
Michael Arlen in *The Green Hat* made a case of syphilis the
raison d'être of his novel, thus making it possible for his
Rolls Royce to be at least six inches longer than most
Rolls Royces. Hemingway's hero in *A Farewell to Arms*
discusses his cured gonorrhea with his lady love. In *Cruel
Fellowship* Cyril Hume gave the same clear-sighted treatment to the homosexual that Radclyffe Hall, an English-
woman, was to give the Lesbian in *The Well of Loneliness*.
Sherwood Anderson had written with fashionable carnality
before the decade began, in *Winesburg, Ohio*, and continued to do so with *Dark Laughter* and *Many Marriages*.
Gertrude Atherton received wide notice for the first
handling of the rejuvenation theme, in the best-selling
Black Oxen. Professor Percy Marks in *The Plastic Age*
interpreted undergraduate capers so vividly that Brown
University decided it could do without his presence in the
classrooms. Many and unpleasant descriptions of natural
functions are scattered through Harry Kemp's *Tramping
on Life*, with carefully careless references to the 'frat
woman' or house prostitute, though the publishers were
cautious enough to print 'son-of-a ——.'

The synthetic, panting passion of E. M. Hull's *The Sheik*
gave many a lonely matron an excited afternoon's reading.
More literate matrons never missed a John Erskine book

after the publication of *The Private Life of Helen of Troy*, in which romantic idols are knocked down irreverently and a bit salaciously. Out of the field of fiction, Marie Saltus in *Edgar Saltus: The Man* told scandalous tales of her dead husband's many love affairs, and wives, his obsessions and phobias, and even his extraordinarily obnoxious brand of baby talk which brought him to call her Mowgy-Puss and when she sailed for Europe to cry: 'Miaw! Wow! Wow! Poor Snippsy goes crazy. O Wowsy wee! Wowsy wee!'

Of the theater of the 'twenties Elmer Rice wrote: 'The serious modern drama in its treatment and discussion of sex is timid, squeamish, superficial, and conventional. . . . It lags far behind the other arts . . . in its attempt to deal sensitively, honestly, and profoundly with the problems of sex.' And as for providing sexual titillation, he maintained it fell far short of newspapers, pulp-paper magazines, and advertisements.

Nevertheless, after literature had paved the way the theater became less timid. *Loose Ankles* was about gigolos, when the male prostitute was just beginning to be spoken of in drawing-rooms. *The Captive*, a French adaptation from Edouard Bourdet, was a standing-room-only sensation, and its performance resulted in a law making dramatic treatment of homosexuality 'obscene' *per se*. In *Lulu Belle* Leonore Ulric as a dusky prostitute sang blues songs, shot craps, and danced a wicked Charleston. *The Unexpected*, a revue, presented a skit called 'Ceinture de Chasteté' from which elderly gentlemen from the country got a thrill and information on medieval birth control. Florence Reed and Mary Duncan were respectively a brothel mistress and a nymphomaniac in *The Shanghai Gesture*. The author, John Colton, was co-author of the adaptation of Somerset Maugham's superb short story, *Rain*, and thus partially responsible for Sadie Thompson's decided and descriptive language which was written into the play. Theatergoers gasped at *White Cargo* when something that was almost a scene of intercourse was staged. *What Price Glory?* was filled with choice and violent remarks, though neither so choice nor so violent as those which rendered *The Front Page* rowdy (the final curtain of the latter falls on 'The son-of-a-bitch stole my watch!').

LESS SEXY SENSATIONS

THERE were other ways of shocking the public than by excessive frankness in dealing with sex, and authors were not slow to find them. Katherine Mayo searched out libelous things about India and wrote her sensational and poorly documented *Mother India*, which provoked two prominent Indians to indignant reply. Kanhaya Lal Gauba produced *Uncle Sham*, which hit hard at our sore spots, the political system, the Ku Klux Klan, the ungodly bigotry of the Church, but puzzled readers by statements quoted from American authorities, such as 'little ones of seven and eight have lovers of about their own age with whom they have sexual intercourse, sometimes in the presence of others.' The scholarly Dhan

Gopal Mukerji more conservatively picked up the cudgels for his country with *A Son of Mother India Answers*.

The Harding régime, which provided enough striking material for a hundred books, was presented sensationally in two non-fiction best-sellers and one book of fiction. *The President's Daughter* by Nan Britton was sufficiently scandalous, the story of a fruitful love affair between Harding and the author.

But *The Strange Death of President Harding* by Gaston B. Means, as told to May Dixon Thacker, outdid this by all odds. In it Means propounded the theory that the Ohio gang which had Harding so under its thumb threatened him with the Britton scandal while they conducted their graft unrestrained. Mrs. Harding, learning of this and fearing the gang was about to break the scandal, preserved the prestige of her husband by killing him, the book hints. The book was a sensation — never had there been such juicy material of White House origin. It had a curious history. Mrs. Thacker after its publication made a statement to the effect that certain facts given her were now proved incorrect, that she had been royally hoaxed. Later she partially repudiated this repudiation.

Samuel Hopkins Adams's *Revelry*, a novel, presented Harding's death as a suicide. In 1922 Harry M. Daugherty, who had a little explaining to do on the subject of his connection with Teapot Dome graft, wrote *The Inside Story of the Harding Tragedy*, which indignantly calls these three books 'scurrilous attacks,' pooh-poohs the idea of Harding's illegitimate child, and that his death was anything other than natural, and winds up magnificently with 'It is yet too early to see him in true, full perspective — a modern Abraham Lincoln whose name and fame will grow with time.'

Church people throughout America grew wroth when Herbert Asbury's *Up from Methodism* appeared. A descendant of the Reverend Francis Asbury, first Methodist bishop ordained in America, and member of a family full of lesser parsons, Asbury's bitter charges against the Church made shocking reading for the faithful. His disgust at the evangelical denominations gave a cutting edge to his denunciations of their dishonesty and viciousness. His descriptions of primitive revival meetings and other churchly activities he was forced to endure in his youth are sickeningly vivid. Much of *Up from Methodism* was printed in *The Mercury*, including the famous 'Hatrack' sketch, and it proved a box-office sensation. Psychologically inclined writers turned out magazine pieces attempting analyses of the man who so violently had turned against all his family had stood for.

The vogue for startling readers extended itself to debunking biographies, causing not only idol-smashing but the setting up of new idols. Traditionally evil individuals — such as Nero, Captain Kidd, Messalina, and Billy the Kid — ceased to be symbols of wickedness. Even Charles J. Finger, the business man turned writer, and editor of the delightful magazine *All's Well*, came out with a book on highwaymen to demonstrate they were not such bad fellows.

To say a thing was so that had not been regarded as so before was a sure way of getting a wide sale. Frederick O'Brien in *White Shadows in the South Seas* reversed the old proverb that white men are degenerated by relations with native women. The personal reputation of the author, combined with the vice-versa thesis he propounded and the sleepy beauty of the book, put it on best-seller lists; it had got around that O'Brien, with graying hair and elegant profile, was the very devil of a fellow, and women fascinated by tales from his smooth Irish tongue were intrigued by the thought of his very personal tours of the South Seas. Unfortunately for O'Brien, such a reputation and such a book leave the author vulnerable to satire, and Doctor Traprock, or George S. Chappell, rose to the occasion as later did Corey Ford to poke unmerciful fun at Joan Lowell and her *Cradle of the Deep*.

'I capture a baby water spout named Gladys, and keep it for a pet.

'I am forced to swim around Cape Horn because Richard Halliburton has exclusive swimming privileges in the Panama Canal.

'HELL'S BELLS! I go to sea at last on the *Île de France*.'

So ran the log of the heroine of *Salt Water Taffy*, with the statements therein only a trifle less absurd than those made by Miss Lowell in perpetrating her literary hoax. Soon after publication an exposure of the fraud was made and it was revealed that Miss Lowell had not lived the first seventeen years of her life on a schooner, spat curves in the wind, nor learned the facts of life from a whale. While all this was supposed to have been going on she made one voyage to Australia and back and occupied the remainder of her time in being a Berkeley, California, schoolgirl. The scandal, instead of causing a boycott, made the book a best-seller.

SELF-PUBLICIZING AND RESULTS

AMY LOWELL'S cry: 'Publicity first; poetry will follow!' was a popular one in the 'twenties. Publishers innovated the informal and usually decidedly silly type of publicity that even in the 'thirties still makes its way to the desks of literary editors. Elizabeth Corbett, author of *Cecily and the Wide World*, let it be known through the medium of her publishing house that she hated 'literature with a purpose, plated silver, free verse, political reformers, and tables that wabble,' and editors permitted this kind of thing to make up the major portion of book columns.

But enterprising authors publicized themselves more dramatically; Floyd Dell became so identified with free love, in spite of his placid life of domesticity, that all his novels were snatched up by eager women thirsting after information on Greenwich Village amours; Josef Washington Hall, who writes under the name of Upton Close, went around Manhattan dressed in a Chinese costume to advertise his *Revolt of Asia*; Waldo Frank in a purple dressing-gown received interviewers in a hotel room draped in purple, explaining that he was in a purple mood that day but that gown and drapes would be changed to another color when his mood veered; Sinclair Lewis from the pulpit of a Kansas City Church called upon God to strike him dead.

Ellen Glasgow, discovering the Younger Generation

boom was leaving her by the wayside and depriving her of sales and prestige, put on a one-woman publicity campaign. Refusing to become 'dated,' this energetic and charming lady mingled at New York literary teas where editors became enchanted with the sparkle of her conversation and departed to give her longer notices than they had intended. Doubleday, Doran devoted more of their advertising budget to her, and when *Barren Ground* was brought out the slogan 'Realism crosses the Potomac' appeared on large advertisements, thereby confusing the large group of Southerners who had been writing as realistically as possible for some years. Miss Glasgow then brushed up her wit, set aside in *Barren Ground*, and produced it at its most ironic in *The Romantic Comedians* and *They Stooped to Folly*. These sold more than satisfactorily. The drive had been a great success.

According to the man who distributes the books of all publishers, however, Miss Glasgow did not mix with the exalted company of those who reached the one hundred thousand mark by six months after publication. Around the middle of the decade some of those writers were Zane Grey, Gene Stratton-Porter, Mary Roberts Rinehart, James Oliver Curwood, Peter B. Kyne, Joseph C. Lincoln, Booth Tarkington, Harold Bell Wright, Dorothy Canfield, Edith Wharton, Frances Hodgson Burnett, Sinclair Lewis, Warner Fabian, and Edna Ferber. Miss Glasgow's books sold very nicely, indeed, but in the company of Willa Cather's, Zona Gale's, Temple Bailey's, and Grace S. Richmond's they missed the wonderfully round figure of one hundred thousand.

Lewis, incidentally, went far beyond this shining goal;

by the end of 1922 *Main Street* had reached three hundred and ninety thousand, and in 1929 it was estimated the book had sold approximately eight hundred thousand copies. With one spruce tree making five hundred books, in 1921 Lincoln's *The Portygee* had demolished seven hundred and fifty trees, Ibañez' *The Four Horsemen of the Apocalypse* six hundred and fifty, Curwood's *The River's End* six hundred, Grey's *Man of the Forest* five hundred and fifty, and Ethel Dell's *Top of the World* six hundred.

Americans traveling in Europe preferred Gertrude Atherton's books to those of other American writers, according to Tauchnitz, the German firm that publishes cheap paper-backed editions of American books, for sale on the Continent only and not to be brought into the United States. In the 'twenties Tauchnitz had brought out twenty-four of her books, seven of Hergesheimer's, three of Lewis's, and two of Edith Wharton's.

Starving wasn't fashionable among literary people. In the 'twenties a successful writer's bank book was as cheerfully full of figures as a successful business man's. For the first time in history big money could be made in writing. The vagaries of Iris March, portrayed by Katherine Cornell on the stage and Greta Garbo in the movies, netted Michael Arlen over one half million dollars, and Hergesheimer is said to have received the same sum for his writings for the *Saturday Evening Post* alone. George Bernard Shaw turned down an offer of one million for the motion-picture rights of all his plays, saying: 'I am not yet convinced that a film version of a play does not seriously depreciate the value of the acting version. It has done so in several cases known to me, and if I go into the filming business at all I shall possibly write especially for the screen.' In 1921 the usual price paid for movie rights of a play was twenty-five hundred dollars to five thousand, rising as high as twenty-five thousand in rare cases.

Production of best-sellers alone, omitting the golden gains received through foreign, movie, theater, and serial rights, started many an author on the way toward the amassing of a modest fortune. The saddening aspect of the matter was that no one knew, or knows now, what makes books sell. Publishers were never sure they had a good thing until the receipts started flowing in. George H. Doran had such little faith in Daisy Ashford's *Young Visiters* that his firm brought out an initial edition of only five thousand copies. Two hundred and fifty thousand had sold three months after publication. The buying public had its moods; occasionally a book would sell a few thousand copies and lapse for long enough for publisher and author to give up hope, then suddenly be catapulted into the upper brackets of best-sellers.

Except in the case of Pulitzer Prize-winners, which automatically become best-sellers, there was rarely a discernible reason for these unexpected buying sprees being concentrated on a single book. The breath of rumor, conversation in a Pullman lounge or on a dance floor, steady press-agenting by a few enthusiasts — no one really knew. Likewise, many an excellent book, heavily pushed and advertised and receiving the plaudits of eminent critics, sold pathetically.

No one could name the proper ingredients that would stir into a best-seller; it was possible to classify the general types of best-selling books — sexy, sweet and light, and so forth — but unclassifiables were constantly putting in an appearance among the money-making few. Entirely different sorts of books would hold the honored place at the head of the list — *Main Street*, Edith Wharton's *Age of Innocence*, Ethel Dell's *Top of the World*, A. S. M. Hutchinson's *This Freedom*, Gertrude Atherton's *Black Oxen*, Lewis's *Babbitt*, *The Little French Girl* by Anne Douglas Sedgwick, Bromfield's *A Good Woman*, *All Quiet on the Western Front* by Erich Maria Remarque. The learned Willard Huntington Wright, writing under the now more famous name of S. S. Van Dine, got *The Bishop Murder Case* on the same list with Lewis's *Dodsworth*; *The Bridge of San Luis Rey* by Thornton Wilder sold widely while Bruce Barton's *What CAN a Man Believe?* and Lindbergh's *We* were doing the same; Temple Bailey's *Wallflowers*, Theodore Dreiser's *An American Tragedy*, and Warwick Deeping's *Sorrell and Son* were popular simultaneously. Emerson Hough's *The Covered Wagon*, the pioneer story that was converted into a movie hit; Christopher Morley's *Where the Blue Begins*, a fanciful parable that children read under the misapprehension it was a dog story; Tarkington's *Gentle Julia*, which delighted Kathleen Norris so that she frightened Pullman car passengers by laughing uncontrollably in the dark of night; Hergesheimer's *The Bright Shawl*, for the filming of which movie people went to Havana and were surprised to find it different from Hergesheimer's thirty-year-ago picture of it; Emil Ludwig's two books named *Bismarck*, titled alike for some reason though brought out by different publishers, one being a biography and one a group of three plays; Anne Parrish's much-applauded *The Perennial Bachelor*, the life and woeful end of a ne'er-do-well — these were some of the diversities on the best-seller scene of the 'twenties.

BOOK CLUBS ARE BORN

IN THE latter part of the decade, however, there arose one method of determining a best-seller. The newly conceived idea of book clubs, organizations sending to their members at established intervals books picked by a judging committee, created an immense and immediate sale for certain books. An author whose book was chosen by one of these clubs could relax happily in the knowledge that he was certain to receive a good sum for his efforts; there was no need for agonizing perusal of sales figures.

But book dealers were not cheered over this new method of distribution. When book clubs were installed a chorus of complaint issued from dealers all over the country. The clubs, they said, were killing their sales. As naturally the clubs were picking what they considered the most sales-worthy books, dealers were being bilked out of their biggest profit items. There were other sour notes. Many persons considered the state of American culture sad enough without the standardization of reading matter that resulted from acceptance of identical literature.

In spite of these laments and mutterings one must conclude that book clubs have improved rather than damaged American literary tastes. Before their advent the problem of distribution seemed insurmountable. In 1920 the United States could boast only two thousand actual book stores. Whole states were without such stores, books being sold over drugstore counters, at news-stands, and in department stores. Denmark, with a population one half that of New York City, contained twelve hundred book shops to New York's three hundred. Although by 1923 fifty million dollars was being spent yearly for chewing gum, it was estimated that only one out of every one hundred and twenty households bought books regularly. Such families, if they lived in a state barren of stores, would buy few, as drugstore selections were small and gaudy. To these persons, of whom there were many thousands, the book clubs came like a gift from heaven. The selections were nearly always admirable, being chosen by learned persons of taste — on the Literary Guild's judging board were Carl Van Doren, Joseph Wood Krutch, and Hendrik Van Loon, and on the Book-of-the-Month Club's Doctor Canby, Christopher Morley, Heywood Broun, Dorothy Canfield, and William Allen White.

These selection committees did not favor shockers — some of their books were W. E. Woodward's *Meet General Grant*, Francis Hackett's *Henry the Eighth*, Lewis Mumford's *Herman Melville*, Claude Bowers's *The Tragic Era*, Ring Lardner's *Round Up*, Du Bose Heyward's *Mamba's Daughters*, Miss Glasgow's *They Stooped to Folly*. In fact, by the time the book clubs were born, shockers had somewhat lost caste. They continued to do so, and by 1930 an author of talents who threw too much low language into his products or gave an unnecessary amount of space to careful description of bedroom pastimes was considered a trifle musty in viewpoint.

The pendulum of taste did not revert to the former prudish position of the pre-'twenties, of course; writers could exercise their skill on practically any subject they chose, and they could handle it in practically any manner they chose. But it had become a little silly to put all you knew about sex into a novel where, likely as not, it affected the working of plot or characterization in no way at all.

IX. THE BOYS GREW OLDER

IX. THE BOYS GREW OLDER

New literary forms always produce new forms of life, and
that is why they are so revolting to the conservative human
mind.

CHEKHOV

PURITANISM and Victorianism were the most frequently walloped but by no means the only punching-
bags of the decade. Novelists were constantly building
up enemies to be demolished by iconoclasm, blasphemy,
and epigram.

Elmer Gantry, Sinclair Lewis's vicious parson, was one.
That preachers like Gantry really exist, probably only the
Methodist Board of Temperance, Prohibition, and Public
Morals would deny, but to argue that the cause of Christianity was demolished, or even critically examined,
when Gantry was exposed as a cad is to argue something
that clearly is not true.

Novels written to ridicule the Elders and their philosophy suffered often from the defect that the villains were
as crudely overdrawn as were the curses-foiled-again
characters of the naïve best-sellers of the 'nineties. They
were written to make out a case, and in consequence
conveyed a sense of unreality, of unfairness, that doomed
them, however highly they were praised upon their appearance, to a certain oblivion. The printed page was not

an invariably satisfying battle field, anyway. If only unconsciously, the rebels felt the need of a test of strength in public conflict.

The trial and execution of two Italians named Sacco and Vanzetti on the charge of robbing a mail truck and killing two persons in the process was as welcome to the intellectuals, therefore, as a thumb placed to the nose is to the tough looking for a scrap. Here was a real enemy. Here was something to wade in and fight about; for the intellectuals not only believed the two laborers were innocent of the crime, but that they were being persecuted because they held radical opinions. The intellectuals saw an extraordinarily vivid shade of red, and they fought, if at times without dignity, with a fervent, unselfish devotion that did them great credit.

The crime for which Sacco and Vanzetti went to the electric chair was committed in Massachusetts on May 5, 1920, and they were arrested three weeks later. At the trial, which began more than a year later, Judge Webster Thayer permitted the prosecution to introduce much testimony that to the lay mind seemed entirely irrelevant, so that, it was argued, it was difficult at times to tell whether the prisoners were being tried for murder, as purveyors of radical literature, as draft-dodgers, or as critics of Harvard. One of them actually was denounced when he remarked he could not send his sons to Harvard because it was a rich man's school.

Judge Thayer's attitude toward the defendants became almost as great an issue as their guilt or innocence. George W. Crocker, a Boston blue-blood, alleged that Thayer had frequently discussed the case with him — an improper act on the part of a jurist — and had expressed great bias against the prisoners. Lois Rantoul, representing the Greater Boston Federation of Churches, said Judge Thayer told her, following testimony in Sacco's favor by his employer, George Kelly, that this testimony was of no consequence because Kelly outside of court had said Sacco was an anarchist. Miss Rantoul said she suggested that only evidence offered in court should be considered, and that Thayer laughed at her. Frank P. Sibley of the Boston *Globe* claimed Thayer remarked of defense attorney Moore, 'I'll show them that no long-haired anarchist from California can run this court.' When the defense on one occasion scored a point, according to Sibley, Thayer said: 'Just wait until you hear my charge! I'll show them.' Robert Benchley, then drama critic of *Life*, quoted Thayer as referring to the defendants as 'those bastards down there,' and saying of defense counsel that he would 'get those guys hanged.' The foreman of the jury was alleged to have told a friend who believed the defendants innocent, 'Damn them, they ought to hang anyway!'

What was the evidence for the state in this *cause célébre*? The most weighty, perhaps, was the identification of Sacco and Vanzetti by witnesses who saw the crime, but this testimony failed to impress those who passionately believed in the prisoners' innocence. Under the ordinary routine of criminal identification, the suspect is lined up with a score or more of persons known to be innocent — usually men who were in prison when the crime was committed — and the witness must pick the guilty one from the group. Sacco and Vanzetti were brought before the witnesses alone, it was claimed, and the witnesses were asked if the two men were the perpetrators of the crime. The defense made much of the fact that the crime took only five minutes and was accompanied, naturally, by a great deal of excitement, but that the witnesses said they were able to make the identification a year later.

The state also produced a ballistics expert who testified that one of the men was shot by a bullet from Sacco's gun, but the defense claimed this testimony was faked. The court of appeals refused to grant a new trial on this evidence, as it did on the confession of a gangster named Celestino Madeiros, who admitted taking part in the crime and claimed it was carried out by the notorious Morelli gang. When the defense asked an appeal on the ground that the prosecuting attorney had suppressed evidence in behalf of the defendants, the Massachusetts Supreme Court ruled: 'A prosecuting attorney is violating no canon of legal ethics in presenting evidence which tends to show guilt while failing to call witnesses in whom he has no confidence or whose testimony contradicts what he is trying to prove.' This opinion was immediately contrasted with clause 5 of the code of ethics adopted by the American Bar Association in 1908: 'The primary duty of a lawyer engaged in public prosecution is not to convict but to see that justice is done. The suppression of facts or the secretion of witnesses capable of establishing the innocence of the accused is highly reprehensible.'

Though the crime had been committed in 1920, it was not until August 22, 1927, that the two men were finally executed. During the interval controversy and passion

THE LITERATI PROTEST

Crowd on Boston Common shortly before Sacco and Vanzetti were executed

were whipped up to an extent unknown since the slavery issue. The intellectuals were enraged by what they considered (many of them have since changed their minds about the case) an effort to suppress free speech and a denial of a fair trial before an impartial judge. They wrote articles and books; they joined the masses in marching, carrying banners, and otherwise 'demonstrating.' Parties in New York where the subject was discussed ended frequently in mass expeditions to Boston, where not a few writers, including Dorothy Parker, Martha Foley, John Dos Passos, and Michael Gold, editor of *The New Masses*, were thrown into jail.

Heywood Broun got into a row with the Pulitzers, owners of the old New York *World*, when they asked him to soft-pedal his blasts against the Massachusetts courts and the governor. The *World* editorially was fighting to have the sentences commuted to life imprisonment, intending later to campaign for a pardon. This seemed to the Pulitzers to be the most sensible strategy, but Broun was hot for release at once. He left the *World* and wrote weekly articles for *The Nation*, though before long he returned to his old position on the page opposite the editorial page.

Felix Frankfurter of the Harvard Law School, later a Roosevelt brain-truster, took up the cause, and wrote a book about it. Upton Sinclair based an indignant novel, *Boston*, on the case, using the transcript of the record for much of his text. Eugene Lyons wrote a definitive account called *The Life and Death of Sacco and Vanzetti*. Babette Deutsch wrote for *The New Republic* a crusading poem called 'Of Sacco and Vanzetti'; and *Can't You Hear*

Their Voices? appeared as the first of the modern propaganda plays.

The magazines and newspapers were full of the case, and even Anatole France addressed, through *The Nation*, an appeal to the American people to save the condemned men. But no protest availed, and the two men finally went to their death, as bombs were exploded in various cities, delegations marched past embassies of the United States in foreign countries, and American intellectuals, weary and angry and disillusioned, got quietly drunk.

THE EVANGELICAL NOVELIST

NEXT to Broun, the most violent and aggressive crusader for Sacco and Vanzetti was Upton Sinclair, who was crusading before many of the young intellectuals were born. Abroad, Sinclair is perhaps the best-known American writer. A hundred and ninety-four translations of his works have appeared in Russia, thirty-six in Germany, thirty in Japan, and smaller numbers in practically all European countries. And yet he does not write to entertain his readers, but to disillusion them about the capitalist system and to convert them to the causes of the masses in the class war which interests him more than anything else save, perhaps, tennis.

Since he gave up writing dime novels, which he began

at the age of fifteen and by which he worked his way through the College of the City of New York, Sinclair has, in his own words, 'written exclusively in the cause of human welfare.' He has 'exposed' one thing after another — the stockyards business in *The Jungle*, the best-seller which netted him enough money to establish the socialist Helicon Home Colony at Englewood, New Jersey; *They Call Me Carpenter*, a novel in which Jesus returns to the earth and is crucified by the American Legion; *The Goose Step*, a blast against American colleges; *The Goslings*, which disposes of the preparatory schools; a denunciation of the press, the oil business, the coal industry, and many others.

Full of reforming zeal, Sinclair is a perennial candidate for office on the Socialist ticket and a battler for the working man, but he would no doubt have gone far as a literary artist if his utopian ideas had not submerged his original ambition to be purely a writer.

A WRITER FAILS TO MILK A COW

THE radicalism of Sinclair, a member of a Southern family of the leisure class whose fortune was swept away in the Civil War, was challenged during the 'twenties by a group of Southerners who likewise were heirs to the best Southern traditions, but who felt quite differently about how to save the world. This group, known variously as 'The Twelve' and 'The Southern Agrarians,' were conservative, violently against every manifestation of political or economic radicalism, and proudly provincial. As the decade ended they appeared, led by John Crowe Ransom, Allen Tate, and the other poets who founded *The Fugitive*, with a manifesto called *I'll Take My Stand: The South and the Agrarian Tradition*, by Twelve Southerners. They had an ambitious program. They argued against the philosophy of industrialism, with its speed, lack of establishment, and insatiable ambitions, and in favor of the older Southern tradition of agrarianism, which fell into eclipse when New England manufacturers began to move their plants below Mason and Dixon's line, where unions were virtually unknown and labor was therefore cheaper.

The Agrarians' argument went like this: The culture of the South was based upon European principles, in that it followed the line of least resistance as to material things. It got its pioneering over with, and lived comfortably in its establishment the only sort of life that can offer leisure, security, and intellectual freedom. Industrialism, on the other hand, is a perpetual pioneering with no recognizable goal, a 'society that is strictly organized for war, but never for peace.' It continues pioneering on principle, without recollection of what pioneering originally was for. 'It is the character of a seasoned provincial life,' wrote Ransom in his essay, 'that it is realistic, or successfully adapted to its natural environment, and that as a consequence it is stable, or hereditable. But it is the character of our urbanized, anti-provincial, progressive, and mobile American life that it is in a condition of eternal flux. Affections, and long memories, attach to the ancient bowers of life in the provinces; but they will not attach to what is always changing.'

I'll Take My Stand was a wholesale offensive against the American gospel of progress, and, coming as the depression was setting in, it got a great deal of attention. Several members of the group were accomplished speakers, and they held debates with industrialists throughout the South, one of them being attended by more than five thousand persons. The dozen essays in the book tackled many phases of the subject — economics, religion, the causes of the Civil War, and so on — and the enthusiastic Twelve planned a magazine and a whole shelf of new books.

But the movement petered out. Ransom and Allen Tate went abroad to write more poetry, an enterprise which interested them more than propagandizing a philosophical and economic movement. And the leaders in the movement eventually came in for much amused spoofing, for it turned out that, although they became lyrical about the agricultural life, none of them really knew anything about it. Andrew Nelson Lytle, the most lyrical, had lived much of his life in New York and Paris, and Starke Young, another member of the group, had been a critic in New York for years. It developed that Stringfellow Barr, who represented industrialism in a debate with Ransom, raised a small vegetable garden, but Ransom had not even once grown a pea. The *reductio ad absurdum* of their paeans to the rural life came when one of the Twelve was confronted with a cow and challenged to milk it. Shuddering in distaste at the thought, he finally admitted he had no idea how to begin.

Significant evidences of the growing up of the younger generation, its recession from the excesses of the first few years of the decade when the revolt was in full swing, are to be found, however, not in 'movements' but in their books. Many of the writers, after straggling for a while, fell out of the line of march, and are heard of no more. Acceptance by publishers and critical welcome came harder in the latter part of the decade than in the first. Gradually the public lost some of its enthusiasm for buying fiction that offered little besides shocking situations, unconventional language, and iconoclasm. Novels had to be better written, to deal with themes other than the search of disillusioned youth for beauty and happiness, to offer greater novelty in material and a more adult attitude toward life.

LOVE AMONG THE CYNICAL

NO YOUNG writer of the decade so completely fulfilled his promise as Scott Fitzgerald. The praise, the flattery, the near-adulation showered upon him when he introduced the younger generation through the romantic haze of *This Side of Paradise* did not turn his head, or make him content to follow the same recipe over and over again. *The Beautiful and the Damned*, published in the early part of 1922, contained most of the virtues and many of the defects of his maiden novel. It too was episodic, badly constructed, at times loosely written, and it likewise depended for its appeal partly upon an impudent and intolerant attitude toward the old folks; the teeth of the clergyman who marries the two leading characters, for instance, are described as 'bourgeois'; and Gloria, visiting General Lee's home, Arlington, becomes annoyed at the sight-seers and exclaims, 'I think it's perfectly terrible, the idea of letting these people come here!' But with the publication of *The Great Gatsby* in 1925 Fitzgerald definitely left the ranks of the experimenters, the bright young men, the *révoltés*, and gave us a mature, well-constructed, and evenly written novel.

That is the mildest praise that could be given *The Great Gatsby*. For once a novel deserved the superlatives of the reviewers. *Gatsby* is a thrillingly beautiful book, and it at once joined Mrs. Edith Wharton's *Ethan Frome* and Hergesheimer's *Linda Condon* among the great fictional works of our literature. Into it Fitzgerald put enough lovely phrases to equip a poet for a lifetime.

It is a novel about extremely unpleasant people, most of them downright cads. Jay Gatz, a penniless young man, raises himself by his bootstraps until, when the war breaks out and he goes to an officers' training camp, he is able to woo a lovely and wealthy Kentucky debutante. While he is in France, she marries rich and boorish Tom Buchanan. Returned from the war, Gatz, who has changed his name to Gatsby, becomes a racketeer and buys a mansion on Long Island, near where Daisy and Tom Buchanan live. Here he gives huge parties, costing tens of thousands of dollars each, to which he invites the whole countryside. He hopes to meet Daisy, whose dock light he can see across the water, and to impress her with his wealth and success. When he finally meets her he tries, unsuccessfully, to get her to leave her husband. Tom meanwhile is sleeping with the wife of a garage keeper. She is killed by a car driven by Daisy, but Tom lets the garage man believe Gatsby was driving the car. The husband kills Gatsby in his swimming pool.

All these people are dishonest in one way or another, and even Jordan Baker, a girl who acts as a foil for the narrator of the story, is accused of having shifted the lie of her golf ball in an important tournament. But Fitzgerald's poetic prose makes their doings seem important and romantic. Gatsby's death, though he was a preposterous hero, becomes quite tragic, and even Daisy, who in a crisis lacked the courage to say she loved Gatsby more than Tom, is a pitiable figure as she retreats into the security of her life of wealth.

With this novel Fitzgerald showed that an easy and cavalier brilliance would not satisfy him, that he was capable of immensely hard work, and that, although he had first won attention as a champion of the post-war generation, he had left their poses, limitations, and naïveté behind him.

FITZGERALD, 7; LEWIS, 7; CABELL, 12

FITZGERALD was the least prolific of the three writers whose startling productions signalized the beginning of the decade. During the 'twenties he produced
only seven books, including three volumes of short stories and his play, *The Vegetable; or, From President to
Postman*, but during the same period James Branch Cabell
turned out twelve and Sinclair Lewis seven, almost any
one of which is as long as Fitzgerald's three novels put
together.

Lewis, in fact, is a man of boundless energy. Burton
Rascoe said of him that 'he can play, dance, and talk all
night, deliver two lectures the next day, and play again
the next night.' Each of his books required as much detailed observation as a writer ordinarily puts into a whole
shelf; *Arrowsmith*, though it was written with the assistance of Doctor Paul de Kruif, required a large knowledge
of medicine before he could begin composition.

Babbitt, the novel which followed the sensational *Main
Street*, was universally regarded as a true portrait of the
small-town, booster type of business man because Lewis
put into it the results of years of observation on service
clubs, of listening to salesmen in Pullman smokers, of
reading press accounts of real estate developments,
crooked municipal politics, chamber of commerce cam-
paigns to transform villages into metropolises, and conventions of Elks, Moose, and other fraternal organizations.

Babbitt, in fact, is an achievement in accurate, complete, and understanding reporting. Its hero is a real estate salesman who lives in a typical suburb with a pathetically unattractive but socially ambitious wife, and believes in all the doctrines to which The Twelve objected — speed, Solid Buick Neighborhoods, the importance of college degrees, a spiritually shabby but outwardly impressive middle-class urban civilization. The novel records Babbitt's fairly successful business career, his one extra-marital sexual adventure, his enthusiasm for Zenith the Zip City, his one revolt against the standards of the life into which he was unwittingly forced, and his final surrender to conformity. The plot is of little consequence, but Lewis whips up a breathless and sustained interest by his fidelity to the details of everyday life, his broad satire, his almost superhuman understanding of his puppets.

Babbitt, which appeared in 1922, was more successful than *Main Street*. It was hailed by the Young Intellectuals as their answer to the demands of an older generation for patriotism, business success, and social respectability. Its sales were tremendous; it became a national issue, with Rotary and Kiwanis luncheon speakers denouncing Lewis as a smart-aleck and a foreigner, while, on the other side of the fence, there were cheers at the unmasking of the self-appointed moral and economic saviors of the country.

Like *Main Street*, *Babbitt* introduced a new word into our language — 'Babbitt' became synonymous with the smug, narrow-minded, overly optimistic, back-slapping small business man — and like *Main Street* it had its uses as an excursion in reform. Business men inveighed against Lewis, but secretly they realized that many of his shafts had struck home — that most members of service clubs, whatever their protestations of altruism, are really banded together for quite selfish business reasons.

The newspapers, outside the book columns, did not dare take sides in the controversy, for too many advertisers were service club members, but criticism became sufficiently general for Rotary, Kiwanis, Lions, Cosmopolitan, and the rest to restrain their more juvenile antics and to take on at least the appearance of organizations composed of mentally adult men. By the end of the decade it was unusual for a Rotary speaker to announce that Christ was the first Rotarian — a frequent theme in the early 'twenties — or for Kiwanians to hold meetings at which members appeared in rompers and rolled hoops and spun tops. Lewis, the reformer who missed the fate of Upton Sinclair, at whose Helicon Hall he once worked as a janitor, and became an artist, thus accomplished, as he had with *Main Street*, the ostensible Rotarian ideal of making America a better place in which to live.

It was three years before Lewis produced his next novel, *Arrowsmith*, and in the course of writing it he was to travel to the West Indies, to South America, and to London. It was finally finished in the château in which George Moore, Lewis's idol, had done much of his writing. It showed a considerable advance over *Main Street* and *Babbitt*. It was less indignant, less a document in reform, more sympathetic in its treatment of human beings. And in it Lewis managed for the first time to create a female character who lives as lustily as Babbitt and Will Kennicott had lived.

After an interlude with *Mantrap*, a near pot-boiler, and *The Man Who Knew Coolidge*, a stunt, Lewis summoned all his old indignation for a colossal wallop at the evangelical clergy. *Elmer Gantry* is the story of a totally despicable hypocrite who uses the Church for what he can get out of it, the while he drinks, keeps mistresses, and violates every taboo he endorses. Gantry is the big business man of religion, climbing to higher and higher triumphs until finally he has New York, and thus the remainder of the country, by the tail. He conceives of a Methodist holding company to take over the Anti-Saloon League, the Lord's Day Alliance, the Board of Temperance, Prohibition, and Public Morals, and other agencies of reform. He would become its head, and thus one of the most powerful men, politically, in the country.

The book is extremely interesting, giving much detail on the trail-hitting racket, but Lewis lays it on too thick. Gantry is not a preacher but a caricature of a preacher, and the Christianity which he expounds is not even Christianity as it is ordinarily known, but a hodge-podge of all its more vicious aspects.

Elmer Gantry marked a distinct backsliding on Lewis's part, but he came back with *Dodsworth*, published in 1929. Lewis had grown more tolerant by the time *Dodsworth* was written, or perhaps he had expended all his wrath upon Gantry, for the man Dodsworth is the type of business man Lewis had not previously admitted existed — kind, honest, intelligent, and interesting as a human being rather than as a freak. *Dodsworth* is the story of the collapse of a marriage, and its principal interest lies in its contrasting of European and American civilizations (not always to the detriment of the American) and the effect upon two Americans of living abroad. Less sensational than his other novels, it is quite possibly his best. Lewis was offered the Pulitzer Prize for writing it, but he turned it down because he objected to the standards of the judging committee.

If Sherwood Anderson's diagnosis is correct, *Dodsworth* had little to do with Lewis's winning of the Nobel Prize, which Lewis did not consider rejecting, for it presented a successful American as a civilized human being. Anderson's theory was that Lewis was given the award because his sharp criticism of American life catered to the dislike, distrust, and envy which most Europeans feel toward the United States. Anderson thought Dreiser should have had the honor, and said so with some bitterness. But, for whatever reason, Lewis got it, and a few months later he went to Stockholm, put on a dress suit, spoke a few words in Swedish, and received, as a sort of proxy for the younger generation whose attitude he so well reflected, the highest honor that can be given a literary man during his lifetime.

FAME IS FICKLE

THE third man behind the explosion of the sunrise gun of the 'twenties likewise survived the decade as a major figure. James Branch Cabell neither won a Nobel Prize nor composed a volume of the tender beauty of *The*

Great Gatsby, but he went on with a procession of books of various kinds that steadily consolidated his eminent position in American letters.

Jurgen was followed two years later by *Figures of Earth*, which treats with all the *Jurgen* tricks of Dom Manuel the Redeemer, the founder of the mythical lineage of the mythical Poictesme with which most of Cabell's books deal. Cabell, in fact, calls his entire shelf of books, excluding the essays and poems, *The Biography of Manuel*, constructing a huge fictional scheme around the conception of life as a comedy forever re-enacted, with birth, ambition, success, love, and death as the forever repeated theme. Jurgen, Dom Manuel, and others inhabit Poictesme, of which Cabell has gone so far as to draw a map, and they are members of a family tree which Cabell has devised to include all his characters from Dom Manuel to Felix Kennaston and John Charteris, the protagonists in his novels of contemporary life. With such skill, in fact, was Cabell's hoax carried out that most readers for years believed he had access to old legends and was using them for his novels and short stories.

Figures of Earth, like the others, contains a weighty foreword discussing its sources, and before each chapter is a passage, supposedly from *Les Gestes de Manuel*, written in such curious English that the innocent reader is likely to rejoice that the legends have been rendered into understandable prose. This introduction, addressed to Sinclair Lewis, was a magnificent piece of spoofing. 'To you (whom I take to be as familiar with the Manuelian cycle of romance as is any person now alive) it has for some while appeared, I know,' wrote Cabell, 'a not incurious circum-

stance that in the *Key to the Popular Tales of Poictesme*
there should have been included so little directly relative
to Manuel himself.' And later Cabell, having quoted in
French a Manuelian authority named Vanderhoffen,
writes: 'Which is quite just, and, when you come to think
it over, proves Dom Manuel to be nowadays, for practical
purposes, at least as real as Doctor Paul Vanderhoffen.'

But in spite of these broad winks, the reading public did
not catch on, and Cabell amused himself by carrying the
fraud further. *The Lineage of Lichfield*, the genealogy
which he invented for his characters, was begun serially in
The Reviewer. Cabell wrote an attack on its authenticity
which he published in *The Reviewer* under another name,
and then, with a show of great indignation, withdrew the
work from its pages, explaining in a letter which *The Reviewer* printed that he could no longer contribute to a
magazine which followed the curious practice of using one
section of the contents to disparage another.

Figures of Earth was a great success, following as it did
the row over the suppression of *Jurgen*, but not very many
years after its publication Cabell's popularity began to
decline. The thoroughly American propensity to create
idols overnight and to forget them as quickly extends to
the reading public, and Cabell felt, though not completely,
its effects. The leading critics of the country continued to
praise each book that he brought out — *The High Place*,
Straws and Prayerbooks, *Something About Eve*, and the
others — but some of the younger critics began to tire of
him. Readers caught on to the Manuelian hoax; the
excitement of the battle of *Jurgen* was forgotten; other
writers offered the combination of sex and irony that had

been the most obvious recommendation of his books to tens of thousands. By the end of the decade he was less frequently discussed than younger writers like Ernest Hemingway and William Faulkner, and three years after the stock market crash he struck the 'James' from the by-line on his volume of essays, *These Restless Heads*, thus announcing a dichotomy between the completed *Biography of Manuel* and 'such other publishings as under the dictates of chance I may or may not emit.'

A MODERN BECOMES VICTORIAN

HEMINGWAY was more than widely discussed; it has been said that by the time he was twenty-five years old he was already 'a myth and a tradition.' Although his output has been small, it is doubtful if any one writer of the period exerted a more profound influence upon his contemporaries. Hemingway, a native of Illinois, went abroad before America entered the war and enlisted in an American ambulance service in France. Later he went to Italy, joined the Ardita, was so severely wounded that he wears a silver plate in one shoulder, and served with such bravery that he was awarded the *Medaglia d'Argento al Valore Militare* and the *Croce di Guerra*, the two highest medals of the country.

Returning to America, he became a reporter on the Toronto *Star*, and later went to France for Hearst. There he began writing fiction, for the Little Magazines, in a style so fresh and effective that he instantly attracted the attention of such men as Fitzgerald and Edmund Wilson. That style was stripped bare; it was hard, simple, direct, staccato. Monotonous when thus described, it was in Hemingway's hands surprisingly flexible, and as he mastered it he turned it to passages of great poetic power.

His alcoholic *The Sun Also Rises* first brought Hemingway to popular attention. It was not until 1929, however (a book of short stories, *Men Without Women*, for the title of which the movies paid five hundred dollars, came in 1927), that Hemingway became established as more than an amusing spokesman for the post-war generation. In that year was published *A Farewell To Arms*, a long and moving novel with the oldest theme in the world — that of a love which ends in the death of one of the lovers.

The story is of an American in the Italian ambulance service who falls in love with an English nurse who cares for him when he is wounded. They fall in love very completely, with a healthy, animal passion. He deserts the army and goes to Switzerland to be with her at the birth of their illegitimate baby. A Caesarean is necessary, and she dies. The book contains scores of long dialogues which consist principally of Catherine and Lieutenant Henry telling each other of their love, and of accounts of the trivial, amusing pastimes with which lovers pass their days. Their romance achieves tenderness by contrast with the coarse, obscene conversation of the soldiers in the camp scenes. So bawdy was the book, in fact, that demands for its suppression were heard, and it was not admitted to many public libraries.

In spite of this, Bertrand Russell, on a lecture tour in America soon after it was published, denounced it as Victorian. And so it was, in the sense that it was a pure love story, but its Victorianism was far different from the tradition which the younger generation had been reviling when the decade opened. It was a Victorianism divorced from all prudery and conventions — a Victorianism purified, as certain critics remarked, by the healthy influence of the post-war generation, its valuable essence extracted and turned to literature that was true to life and hence worthy of survival.

One of the most promising literary talents of the generation, Hemingway was equally interesting for the influence he exerted over his contemporaries. He was imitated before he was known to any large percentage of novel-writers, and men like Morley Callaghan, author of *Strange Fugitive*, and Charles Wertenbaker, author of *Boojum* and *Peter the Drunk*, show his influence. About Hemingway, who described himself as principally interested in 'skiing, fishing, shooting, and drinking,' there are enough stories afloat to outfit his biographer, if he ever has one, handsomely. One is that he saved John Dos Passos from being killed in a bullfight. Another is that, enraged at the foul blows struck by a boxer in a bout at the Salle Wagram in Paris, he entered the ring and knocked out the champion.

Hemingway and Faulkner were the two brightest literary stars that rose during the latter half of the decade. They have little else in common — unless it is their shared hatred for New York. Hemingway dislikes even to pass through the metropolis to get a boat. Faulkner's publishers spent months trying to lure him there for a round of literary teas, and when he arrived he spent the entire visit in a friend's apartment, refusing to budge for the parties arranged in his honor.

REVOLT IN PETTO

A S HERBERT ASBURY turned on the Methodism of his ancestors, Faulkner rejected the romanticism of his. Of a Southern family which included governors and generals, he is the great-grandson of the William Faulkner who wrote *The White Rose of Memphis*, a popular romantic novel. Faulkner is the most important of the Southern writers who have fled from the tradition of an aristocratic romanticism. His first novel, *Soldier's Pay*, produced in 1926 (he had published a volume of poems two years before), dealt realistically with the homecoming of a soldier who had been reported killed in action.

This novel attracted wide attention in England, but it was not until 1929, with *The Sound and the Fury*, that Faulkner was seriously considered in America. The story deals with the decay of a Southern family as seen through the eyes of an idiot son. It reveals an obsession with the morbid, the pathological, the vicious that recalls Dostoevsky. In the early 'thirties Faulkner repeated the formula with several strange, curiously beautiful, and, to some, revoltingly morbid novels. Now successful, he no longer had to paint houses to supplement his literary income.

The literary renaissance in the South was distinguished by a revolt of its own — a revolt against the Southern literature of tradition. Typified by the novels of Thomas Nelson Page and John Esten Cooke, this literature had been compounded of shining swords, mellow words under the moonlight, the sweet colored mammy, colonels, and the noble loves of the aristocracy. The South, which followed Chicago as the most literary region of the country, in the 'twenties began to produce novels that were intensely 'realistic' like T. S. Stribling's, morbid like Faulkner's, or satirical like Isa Glenn's, Sara Haardt's, or Ellen Glasgow's.

Miss Glenn, a Georgian whose principal debunking of the Southern legend and tradition was *Southern Charm*, did not begin her literary career until 1927, but Miss Glasgow, one of the best thought-of novelists of our times, has been in revolt against the Southern tradition of sentiment and the system of chivalry in which a woman's education 'was designed to paralyze her reasoning faculties' during her entire career, which began in 1897 with the publication of *The Descendant*. In preparation for writing her second novel, *The Voice of the People*, she managed to get into a state political convention, an extremely daring achievement for a woman in those days. In 1925, when *Barren Ground* was published, Miss Glasgow decided that what the South needed was 'blood and irony,' and in her succeeding social satires — *The Romantic Comedians* and *They Stooped to Folly* — she played an amusing and devastating stream of irony upon the old colonel tradition.

THE PETTICOATED WING

MISS GLASGOW'S chief rival as a fictional ironist was another woman, Anne Parrish, the most celebrated writer Colorado has produced. Miss Parrish's second novel, *Semi-Attached*, published in 1924, had precisely the theme one would expect of a writer coming to literary age at that time: it assumed that marriage was necessarily a dreadful business, it endorsed immorality, and it presented a woman in the unromantic rôle of pursuer.

This theme has little to offer other than its element of shock, but with *The Perennial Bachelor*, published the following year, Miss Parrish produced a mature work that belonged not to the decade but, as enthusiastic critics cried, to Literature. This novel, which took the two thousand dollar Harper Prize, deals with a man's entire life, from the time he is a petted and indulged child until, at the age of sixty, he is still rushing the debutantes, who hardly conceal their contemptuous amusement. The portrait of him is devastating — he is a self-centered, pleasantly stupid, and utterly worthless person — but Miss Parrish's full wrath is reserved for the mother and the sisters who submerge their lives in his and devote to him the lion's share of the dwindling family income.

Mencken once said that if a woman ever told the truth, the whole truth, about women, the book would amaze the world. Miss Parrish did not do this, nor did she undertake to do it, but she showed us women as few men, if any, have been able to do.

Mencken has also said that women should some day take the leadership in novel-writing away from men. There are plausible reasons why they should. They are shrewder than men in discerning motives, they are privy to subtleties in human relationships of which men are quite unaware, and, most important, they understand one half of the human race with a thoroughness that is beyond most men. In the 'twenties women did not achieve the leadership Mencken had predicted would inevitably be theirs, but there was a long and imposing list of women writers. One of the more spectacular successes was Elizabeth Madox Roberts, who in 1926 with her first novel, *The Time of Man*, moved Sherwood Anderson to walk to a telegraph office and wire her publishers: 'I am humble before her genius.' This story of poor whites in the Kentucky hills challenged *The Great Gatsby* as a poetic novel.

In her deep study of people Miss Roberts resembles Willa Cather, who joins Miss Glasgow and Edith Wharton to form the trinity that dominates the feminine wing of American literature. Miss Cather, though she was born in Virginia, so loves the prairie lands and their people, among whom she was raised, that when she lived in France homesickness drove her into the wheat fields to weep. As a child she played with the children of immigrants — Swedish, Bohemian, German, French, and Russian — and as she grew older she sensed a poetic dignity in their struggles to earn a living in their adopted homeland. She left the Middle West only because it could not give her the advantages, principally concerts, which she demanded, and even now her best friends are those she made in Nebraska, Wyoming, and the other states she loves so well. Never spectacular in her themes or treatment, Miss Cather was slower in winning recognition than many of her contemporaries, but her reputation — founded principally on *My Antonia*, *A Lost Lady*, and *Death Comes for the Archbishop* — is so secure that she has been mentioned for the Nobel Prize. George Jean Nathan considers her the finest stylist in America.

Mrs. Wharton, the third of the trinity, is a member of an aristocratic New York family and has roamed widely in the field of fiction. What is undoubtedly her finest work — the brief *Ethan Frome*, a tragedy of love and frustration which is Grecian in its form — is about New England folk. *The Age of Innocence*, winner of the Pulitzer Prize in 1920, deals with the old New York society in which she was raised. She has written travel books on France, where she fed and housed six hundred Belgian refugee orphans during the war, Italy, and Morocco, which she visited upon the invitation of Marshal Lyautey. Versatile and well-to-do, she has worked almost as hard at literature as a penny-a-liner for his bread and meat. Always slightly missing greatness, save with *Ethan Frome*, she has contributed a distinguished shelf of books to American literature — books that are always well-bred and which never fail to reveal her high admiration of Henry James, who once said of her, after reading an early story, that he wanted 'to get hold of the little lady and pump the pure essence of my wisdom and experience into her.'

AN ELDER IS ANNOYED

M RS. WHARTON was one of several writers who
went through the 'twenties almost unmoved by the
currents that swirled about them. Booth Tarkington, who
said in the early part of the decade that he had never
heard of the Young Intellectuals, almost succeeded in
ignoring them, but in 1927 he was stirred to ridicule them
in *The Plutocrat*.

The Plutocrat is set on a Mediterranean cruise, among
the tourists on which is a complacent representative of the
younger generation who has just had a play produced on
Broadway. Written for 'the few' and intended to be very
'searching' — a word with which Tarkington has much
fun — it turns out to be immediately popular. (Though
he despises the masses, Laurence Ogle is not averse to
accepting their money.) On the cruise is a capitalist who
represents all he detests. Mr. Tinker is rich, hearty, in-
sensitive to 'the finer things.' The play collapses suddenly
and Ogle finds himself in North Africa with only sixty-
seven dollars. After great spiritual travail and humiliation,
he decides to borrow from Tinker. But about this time he
falls in love with Tinker's daughter, and this source of
loan is closed. Tarkington despises Ogle, and emphasizes
Tinker's superiority throughout the book, but he does not
let his prejudice take him to the point of having Ogle
borrow the money. His agent sells the play to the movies,
a fat check arrives, and Ogle is saved the ultimate degra-
dation. Tarkington even lets him marry the girl.

Had Tarkington's blast against the Young Intellectuals appeared earlier in the decade, he would have been torn, figuratively, limb from limb. As it was, there were critics who denounced him for glorifying a business man at the expense of a writer, and when Tarkington later advised the young not to drink, after a gay youth and middle age in which he is said to have consumed his quota of high-balls, these critics gleefully said that he was just an old bourgeois hypocrite, anyway.

Tarkington cannot be dismissed so easily. He hardly ranks with Miss Cather, or Dreiser, or Cabell. 'He is always,' wrote Mencken, 'on the verge of a first-rate book, but just missing it.' But he has never written a really shoddy book. He has an almost divine gift for story-telling. His style is easy, his construction so adept that one is never aware of it, as one occasionally is in, say, the short stories of Wilbur Daniel Steele. He gives the impression of great wisdom, maturity, and tolerance. And he is gifted with the lightness and grace of a Henry Harland.

DREISER LUMBERS ON

THEODORE DREISER, like Tarkington, produced most of his best work before the decade began, but, unlike Tarkington, he was, without volition, a major literary figure of the 'twenties. Since the publication of his first novel, *Sister Carrie* in 1900, Dreiser has been hunted by the censors, the Puritans, and the professors. Though less sexy than Anderson and many other writers, Dreiser has always been considered a bad influence for the young. The protests against *Sister Carrie* were so vehement that the publishers voluntarily withdrew it, and for eleven years Dreiser was silent. His second novel, *Jennie Gerhardt*, was his masterpiece. It has been called the greatest tragedy in American literature, and there is no doubt that in the scene in which Jennie, the mistress of the wealthy hero whom she could not marry, steals into church for his funeral, afraid to speak to his high-hat family, is as moving as anything in any literature.

Dreiser's aim was to make the novel true to life, and the writers who were influenced by him finally threw off the yoke of the peaches-and-cream tradition that flourished when he began writing. *Jennie Gerhardt* was not suppressed, but *The Genius*, which came four years later and also dealt with illicit love, fell under the axe. When the 'twenties arrived, Mencken was whooping it up for him with such fervor that all the Young Intellectuals became aware of him. He became a sort of symbol of revolt, a rallying-point for the fight against Victorianism and Puritanism.

In the 'twenties he produced *A Gallery of Women*, a book of sketches, and *Dreiser Looks at Russia*. He went to Russia to 'revise my understanding of America.' The account of his impressions contained passages which were identical with passages from a book that had just been written by Dorothy Thompson, Sinclair Lewis's new wife. At a dinner in New York Lewis charged him with plagiarism, and Dreiser, although approaching sixty, slapped his face.

An American Tragedy, a massive double-decker, was his principal work of the decade, and this, too, was barred by certain libraries. The story, based upon a sensational murder trial, is of a young man's rise in the world to the point where he feels he cannot afford to marry the commoner whom he has got with child. He takes her boating and drowns her, pretending it was an accident. He is tried, convicted, and executed.

This novel exhibits all of Dreiser's virtues and defects. As a piece of writing, it is undoubtedly the worst book ever taken seriously in America. Dreiser never wrote well for more than a few sentences at a time, but in *An American Tragedy* he sunk to depths that are almost inconceivable in a literate man. And yet, in spite of its bungling phraseology, its endless repetition of colorless and harsh words, its appalling monotony of sentence structure, the story and emotion finally take form and become breathtaking and moving. Dreiser, in his clumsy style, piles up thousands upon thousands of words to describe an object or a feeling, but somehow or other he always gets his effects. 'His great lumbering imagination,' wrote Llewelyn Powys, 'full of divine curiosity, goes roaring through the prairie-lands of the Cosmos with the restless, heavy-shouldered force of an old bull *wildebeest*.' And William Marion Reedy, who edited the excellent *Reedy's Mirror* in St. Louis before the 'twenties, said: 'Thank God, Dreiser hasn't got a style. If he ever gets one it's good-bye.'

It is now much too late to fear — or hope — that he will develop a style. But however much one may wish that he wrote better, there is a general agreement that his other qualities outweigh this deficiency. His tolerance for human frailty, his genuine love for humanity — not a maudlin expression, but a genuine indignation against injustice — are sweeping; one feels that his heart is big enough to hold the world. As he approaches the end of a life of struggle, disappointment, antagonism and achievement in the face of every handicap, there is something majestic about him — lonely, honest, understanding, pitying, disillusioned, and yet hopeful as a child is hopeful that on some distant tomorrow life will be more nearly tolerable for sensitive men.

In 1928 a magazine editor asked Dreiser for a brief expression of his philosophy, and in one of the few passages of fine writing he has done he gave the world what must be the final word on his life:

> I can make no comment on my work or on my life that holds either interest or import for me. Nor can I imagine any explanation or interpretation of any life, my own included, that would be either true or important, if true. Life is to me too much of a welter and play of inscrutable forces to permit, in my case at least, any significant comment. As I see him the utterly infinitesimal individual weaves among the mysteries a floss-like and wholly meaningless course — if course it be. In short, I catch no meaning from all I have seen, and pass quite as I came, confused and dismayed.

X. SOBERING UP

X. SOBERING UP

At the end of 1930, as compared with the previous year, average commodity prices had dropped 18 per cent; the price of wheat had fallen 45 per cent; cotton, 45 per cent; copper, 47 per cent; rubber, 55 per cent; silver bullion, 32 per cent; car loadings had decreased 13 per cent; steel production, 27 per cent; automobile production, 40 per cent; payments by bank checks, 25 per cent.

HACKER AND KENDRICK: *The United States Since 1865*

THE financial *débâcle* of late '29 and early '30 brought most of us back to fundamentals as suddenly and harshly as if we had all been jailed after a glorious tear. Landing with a jar, we scanned the scene and found that mysterious statistical phenomena were exerting a potent influence on our destinies. One of them, car loadings, unknown to esthetes in the 'twenties, were discovered to be most important and to be fewer with each report. Stock-market averages, a more familiar index, fell into a steady decline, after a few hopeful, desperate rallies. Banks began to fail, factories to shut down, bread-lines to stretch longer and longer — and finance companies took away from us the radios, the electric refrigerators, the automobiles, and even the homes we had bought 'on time' in the happy belief that credit could be expanded forever.

Before long the extravagances of the 'twenties seemed as far off as the fairy world of childhood. By the time the Decade of the Depression dawned we thought incredulously, or enviously, or with a touch of shame of our follies and good-fellow sprees and delusions — the Lindbergh reception, flagpole-sitting, five-million-share days, Two Cars in Every Garage and a Chicken in Every Pot. But we did not think of them very often, for grubbing for a living was becoming a full-time job, and we were learning to take our fun where we could find it.

WRITERS TURN ECONOMISTS

THE depression closed the decade as dramatically as, from a literary point of view, it had begun, and it ended talk of the revolt as it ended our dreams of banishing poverty from the land. When the 'thirties arrived, writers were working feverishly to learn the definitions of such phrases as 'a flight of capital' and to master problems like the relation of heavy goods manufacture to consumer income. The magazine and the book buying public wanted economics in articles and stories — something to explain the catastrophe that had shaken every individual in America. Novels were written around the stock-market crash of October 24, 1929. Others dealt with the efforts of once wealthy families to adjust themselves to privation and unemployment. Writers became conscious of the class struggle and other economic and political philosophies than the American, and a few of them became Communists. The Quality Group of magazines was more interested in discourses on economic panaceas and bold articles on the technique, possibilities, and potentialities of revolution in America than in any other theme. Stuart Chase quickly became a popular writer — an unheard-of achievement for an economist — and other authors plunged into the dismal science to keep him and his imitators from cornering the market in magazine articles and non-fiction books.

Not all of them, of course. Kathleen Norris wrote 'advice' pieces for her huge feminine following, telling wives to help their husbands bear their reverses by being brave and smiling. Erskine Caldwell turned to the beaten, hopeless share-croppers of the South. But for every Norris, Caldwell, Chase (and even Eddie Cantor, who recouped his stock-market losses with a humorous book called *Caught Short*), there were a dozen writers, mostly novelists, who showed in their work no awareness of the depression.

'COME THE REVOLUTION'

THERE were others who took advantage of it to win a hearing which they could not have got during the boom.

It was perhaps characteristic of Americans that when the depression came we were more bewildered and frightened than any other people in the world would have been under comparable adversity. Lacking the emotional and intellectual stability of older and more homogeneous peoples — lacking, as a specific example, the Englishman's allegiance to tradition — we felt that the day of doom was nigh unless we did something radical and revolutionary to ward it off. Instead of pulling in our belts and 'muddling through,' as did Britain and Sweden, instead of dealing with the agricultural problem in a sane and practicable manner, as did France, we thought in terms of throwing overboard all we had learned about government and economics. Panaceas like Technocracy became as popular as new preventives for colds.

In the stir and unrest a moderately sized buying public appeared for a group of writers who called themselves Proletarian artists. A Proletarian writer was one who concerned himself with what was once known as the 'seamy side of life.' Writers have always written of the economically downtrodden — Dreiser is an important American example — but the Proletarians added something to the formula.

This ingredient was the doctrine of revolution. Their purpose was that of the propagandist. In many novels the propaganda for Communism or an approach to it was expressed in long editorial passages which slowed up the story; in other cases, somewhat more subtly, it vilified the successful and glorified the downtrodden. These novels, short stories, and articles sought to arouse class hatred by painting harrowing pictures of reform schools, life among the garment workers, police brutality toward strikers.

Americans, looking restlessly for a short cut to economic salvation, bought Proletarian novels in sufficient quantities for their publication to be profitable. The anti-

Acme

PROLETARIAN LITERATURE IS BORN
Scene outside the New York Stock Exchange during the 1929 *débâcle*

capitalistic movement in letters was just getting under way as the decade ended, but by the middle of the 'thirties it was sufficiently extensive for Granville Hicks to issue an anthology of *Proletarian Literature in the United States*.

Hicks's book revealed not only that the movement had failed to produce a single piece of moderately good writing, but that the Proletarians have no standard of criticism which an artist would recognize. (A writer in *The New Masses*, instructing Proletarian book critics, solemnly said that Admiral Byrd's book on his South Pole expedition should be attacked on the ground that Byrd named newly discovered land after American capitalists.) Hicks dismissed as worthless or nearly so Edith Wharton, Dreiser, Fitzgerald, Mencken, O'Neill, James Huneker, Robert Frost, Lewis, Cabell, Hergesheimer, Edwin Arlington Robinson, and Irving Babbitt. As the glories of American literature he listed Michael Gold, Grace Lumpkin, Isidor Schneider, Josephine Herbst, Clifford Odets, Alfred Maltz, and Albert Halper.

The only assumption to be drawn from Hicks's amazing classification is that his enthusiasm for political and economic revolution had destroyed any literary standards he may have once possessed. That the Proletarians have produced nothing to warrant comparison with the average output of the writers they condemn is, as Ernest Boyd remarked with commendable mildness, 'an obvious matter of ordinary literary judgment.'

POSES FALL AWAY

A S THOUGH by common consent, the non-Prole-
tarian writers left their revolt behind them as the
decade ended. It had almost petered out when the panic
hit, anyway, but the panic cut as definite a dichotomy in
our national life as the demarcation in literature created
by the almost simultaneous appearance of *Main Street*,
Jurgen, and *This Side of Paradise*. Problems that seemed
important before General Electric dropped from 296 to
168 appeared to be trivial afterward. When Herbert
Hoover was inaugurated as President his message to the
people named the enforcement of prohibition as the most
important problem before the country. Four years later,
when Franklin Roosevelt took office, he did not mention
prohibition. If he had, regardless of whether he favored or
opposed it, the issue would have seemed too petty to
consider. The depression's curious effect of reassorting
values extended to literature, and for writers as the decade
ended to have gotten fussed about Puritanism and
Victorianism would have seemed not merely supereroga-
tory but something of a *faux pas*.

Clearly the writer's cue was to settle down to serious
work, leaving the poses, the belligerence, the persecution
and superiority complexes of his holiday behind him.
Puritanism, certainly, in so far as it was represented by
censorship, had been almost vanquished. The writer was
free to talk of sex or the natural functions of the body, if

his theme called for it. With very few exceptions, he could write in the language of the gutter. John S. Sumner and a few other crusaders still functioned, but in so feeble a condition that they were objects of commiseration rather than rage.

Victorianism was reviled so thoroughly at the beginning of the 'twenties that no young writer or collegian of intellectual leanings would have admitted the long age of the good and simple Queen had had any virtues whatsoever. But a movement so unsubstantial as that against Victorianism was headed for an early collapse. After all, there were the solid, unassailable achievements of the Victorians. Even Fitzgerald, one of their hardiest adversaries, admired Algernon Charles Swinburne to the extent of quoting him and imitating him in the fugitive verse in *This Side of Paradise*. Gradually it dawned on even the most hostile of the young that one could not argue that Darwin was an insignificant figure in human progress because his contemporaries made uncomfortable chairs, or that Newman wrote badly because he lived in an age of prudery, or that Rossetti was a fifth-rate poet because the women he knew wore a ridiculous number of petticoats. Victorianism began to take on a definition that had more sense in it and more basis in truth, and this clearer understanding destroyed some of the excuse for the angry insurrection. When the generation had won the right to candor in speaking and writing, and had achieved some of the comforts in what Eddie Guest called 'just livin'' which the conventions of the nineteenth century had prohibited, the revolt had achieved all that was worth achieving. The young and the by now younger generation began to view the great Victorians without the blinkers of prejudice. In the book reviews of even the very young, they ceased to be mentioned in the tone customarily used in referring to horse thieves.

The revolt was over. The mention of Victorianism no longer raised blood pressures, nor did Puritanism as it was interpreted in the early part of the decade cause a clenching of fists and a resolve to do or die for Freud. The stream of finances drying up at the source, expatriates returned to New York, to Des Moines, and to Dallas, with memories of days that were to seem increasingly wicked and glamorous as middle age approached. The Negro movement was dead, books by Negroes being regarded again on their merits, with a consequent diminution in the trips of dusky scribblers to the savings account windows of the banks. Dadaism was dead, and Tristan Tzara was recalled only as a monumental joke. Expressionism was dead, Vorticism was dead. The Little Magazines which dotted the literary scene by the scores in the early 'twenties were now far fewer in number, and soberer — published like commercial magazines under the necessity of giving readers something for their money besides the egotism of editors.

CODA WITH SOFT PEDAL

THE decade ends, then, with the literary world far less exciting than it was when Scott Fitzgerald first told us about petting in parked cars, when Mencken chased the professors to the campus libraries, and when Cabell described a seduction in terms that launched a thousand blushes. The Proletarians offered nothing to take the place of this. The young no longer dominated the scene, for the reason that high positions tended to be held by those who got them in the early 'twenties, and these executives were no longer very young. There were fewer idle, quasi-literary sophomores to admire them. Sophomores had less time for literary teas and less inclination to spend their time on pursuits which would not increase their capacity to earn a living after graduation. And with U-Drive-It garages in college towns failing by the hundreds, it was apparent the collegians no longer had money to spend on new fiction and tall paper, limited editions.

The literary world at the end of the decade was less exciting, but there was no longer need for any great shouting and rushing about and waving of arms. The revolt, for all its excesses and stridency, had been, as the Wall Streeters so frequently said of business when the stock market was tumbling, 'fundamentally sound.' Its achievement was magnificent in the direction of liberating the writer from most of the restrictions that had hampered him in the free pursuit of his artistic aims and in his efforts to portray contemporary life and thought faithfully. In fact, the writer got his Magna Charta, his Declaration of Independence, and his Bill of Rights during the decade. He was free to prove that he was worthy of them, that he had been censor-hunting not merely for the sport of it but because he wanted to say something worth while that the censors were keeping him from saying.

What really died in the literary world when the 'thirties came was the externals of the writing profession, the over-emphasis on social life, the squabbles with representatives of an older tradition, the clash of movements, the fight for recognition of the Negro, censor-baiting, debates as to whether the South or the Middle West was the most productive section of the country from the point of view of letters. With these diversions and distractions out of the way, writers had the time and the freedom for great work.

The future was theirs.

THE END

INDEX

INDEX